Twelve Stones of Grace

The Story of Dr. Aletta G. Bell

By Nicky McMaster

Edited by Carla Myers
carlamyersediting.com

Twelve Stones of Grace
Copyright © 2025 by Nicole McMaster.

All rights reserved. No part of this publication may be reproduced, distributed, or transmitted in any form or by any means, including photocopying, recording, or other electronic or mechanical methods, without the written consent of the publisher. The only exceptions are for brief quotations included in critical reviews and other noncommercial uses permitted by copyright law.

MILTON & HUGO L.L.C.
4407 Park Ave., Suite 5
Union City, NJ 07087, USA

Website: *www. miltonandhugo.com*
Hotline: *1- 888-778-0033*
Email: *info@miltonandhugo.com*

Ordering Information:
Quantity sales. Special discounts are granted to corporations, associations, and other organizations. For more information on these discounts, please reach out to the publisher using the contact information provided above.

Library of Congress Control Number:	2025915422
ISBN-13: 979-8-89285-460-3	[Paperback Edition]
979-8-89285-461-0	[Hardback Edition]
979-8-89285-459-7	[Digital Edition]

Rev. date: 07/31/2025

Scripture quotations marked (NLT) are taken from the Holy Bible, New Living Translation, copyright ©1996, 2004, 2015 by Tyndale House Foundation. Used by permission of Tyndale House Publishers, Carol Stream, Illinois 60188. All rights reserved.

Scripture quotations marked (CEV) are from the Contemporary English Version Copyright © 1991, 1992, 1995 by American Bible Society. Used by Permission.

Scripture quotations marked (GNT) are from the Good News Translation in Today's English Version- Second Edition Copyright © 1992 by American Bible Society. Used by Permission.

Scripture quotations marked (ERV) are taken from the HOLY BIBLE: EASY-TO-READ VERSION © 2001 by World Bible Translation Center, Inc. and used by permission.

Scripture quotations marked (NIV) are taken from the Holy Bible, New International Version®, NIV®. Copyright © 1973, 1978, 1984, 2011 by Biblica, Inc.™ Used by permission of Zondervan. All rights reserved worldwide. www.zondervan.comThe "NIV" and "New International Version" are trademarks registered in the United States Patent and Trademark Office by Biblica, Inc.™

Scripture quotations from the COMMON ENGLISH BIBLE (CEB). © Copyright 2011 COMMON ENGLISH BIBLE. All rights reserved. Used by permission. (HYPERLINK "http://www.commonenglishbible.com/"www.CommonEnglishBible.com).

*For the displaced, defenceless, and vulnerable.
May those who are homed, protected, and safe help you.*

*And for my Gran, Jessie Evelyn McMaster,
who loved and nurtured me from my first breath to her last.*

FOREWORD

The word heroic is overused in our day.

We say a quarterback is heroic if he leads a fourth-quarter comeback. We call a politician heroic if he wins the election after losing it the first time around.

But what makes a hero?

It must be something like this. An ordinary person, raised in ordinary circumstances, rises above the fray and does something important that no one expected.

Seen in that light, Aletta Bell is a hero, and her life is heroic.

At one point in this book, she mentions the time Marlene and I traveled from Chicago to India to spend a few days with her at the Duncan Hospital in Raxaul, in the Bihar province. Everything she says about our visit is true.

Thirty years later, this is what I remember. The poverty was overwhelming, and the dirt was everywhere. When

FOREWORD

Aletta led us to our room, she showed us how to get hot water for a shower by putting a heating coil in a bucket of water.

When we saw her apartment, it was small, even tiny by American standards. But one thing has stayed with me over the years. She was so cheerful in circumstances that, for most Americans, would seem impossible to endure.

Aletta smiled and laughed and understood our difficulty because years earlier, she had come to India to serve as a medical missionary.

This book tells the story of her amazing journey from Canada to the US to India to the ends of the earth. None of it was planned in advance, but nothing happened by chance. Aletta Bell set out to serve the Lord, step by step, following God's leading. She waited on the Lord; he opened the doors, and with faith and zeal and infectious enthusiasm, she went through those doors.

Each chapter is a "stone" in the memorial of her life's work. Together those stones are built as an altar to the Lord. They show us what one person can do whose life is yielded to God.

As one who knew Aletta Bell and who caught a glimpse of her work, I can tell you that this book is the heroic story of what one woman can do. More than that, every page testifies to the faithfulness of God, who led her all the way.

Let's settle in as we relive Aletta Bell's incredible journey. It began more than eighty years ago on a farm near a small town in Ontario.

But as you will see, it doesn't end there.

May God use this book to inspire you to follow Jesus wherever he leads!

Ray Pritchard
President, Keep Believing Ministries

CONTENTS

Foreword ix
Preface xv
Family 1
Faith 23
Foundation 37
Fellowship 61
Focus 87
Foreign Field 109
Freedom 151
Faithfulness 173
Friction 187
Fruit 231
Forward 263
Future 283

PREFACE

So Joshua called together the twelve men he had chosen—one from each of the tribes of Israel. He told them, "Go into the middle of the Jordan, in front of the Ark of the LORD your God. Each of you must pick up one stone and carry it out on your shoulder—twelve stones in all, one for each of the twelve tribes of Israel. We will use these stones to build a memorial. In the future your children will ask you, 'What do these stones mean?' Then you can tell them, 'They remind us that the Jordan River stopped flowing when the Ark of the LORD's Covenant went across.' These stones will stand as a memorial among the people of Israel forever."

Joshua 4:4–7 (NLT)

PREFACE

----Original Message----

From: Nicky McMaster
Sent: December 4, 2015, 7:47 p.m.
To: Aletta Bell
Subject: Writing your story.

. . . You have had a great life. Your story begins with a simplicity and isolation that not many would fathom as belonging to you. From poverty and being last in the line of nine children, God took your hand in His and led you on an unimaginable journey! And it's not over yet!

As your hair has greyed and your work has lessened, people are pestering you to unravel your life into print. I am one of them. Perhaps you underestimate the value of your stories. In their telling, you always weave the wisdom, compassion, and power of God's ways. Much like the stories you listened to as a child that planted God's seed in your heart, your stories also encourage and empower.

Dr. Bell, you do realize that I am not qualified to write your story? My grammar is unrefined, and my native land is on the underside of the globe. But I am willing to help you. If you are willing to speak your story, I am willing to write it down for you. Your story needs no embellishment; it just needs to be written.

I am passionate about broken lives being transformed. Your story told in truth with the intensity in which it was lived will change lives. It may persuade others to act and to reach the unreached—to tell them that no matter what their beginnings, they are loved because nothing can separate them from the love of God...

From: Aletta Bell
Sent: Saturday, December 5, 2015, 5:21 a.m.
To: Nicky McMaster
Subject: RE: Writing your story.
   ... No, I don't underestimate the value of my stories because they show God's tremendous love, grace, and power. And yes, I need you to help me get them down on paper. People are fascinated when I talk about my adventures, but I can't write about them. I can talk about them as that is not so permanent as writing them for all to see...

It was most definitely *not* on my bucket list to sell an investment property, resign from my job in Australia, fly to the United States, meet up with an almost eighty-year-old retired medical doctor, and travel with her (without an itinerary) to write her biography. Dr. Bell and I were born in opposite hemispheres: I in Australia and she in Canada. Our paths first crossed in 1994 when, travelling under the banner of her charity, Dr. Bell spoke at various gatherings in Australia, encouraging youth to join her in her service. In my eyes, she was formidable. As much as I longed to join her in India, or even make my aspirations known, I was too afraid to introduce myself.

PREFACE

A year later, at twenty-three, I joined an international charity as a short-term associate to work as a nurse in India. It was my first trip outside of my home country, the coming together of childhood ambitions, shaped by the life of Gladys Aylward (a British missionary to China portrayed in the movie *The Inn of the Sixth Happiness*). Aylward's courage and firmness of purpose left an indelible mark on my ten-year-old heart.

During my stay in India, the evening meal was a communal event for short-term workers. Dr. Bell sat at the head of the table. Sometimes she would tell us stories of her life and adventures. Inspired, I kept a journal, writing as much as I could remember and marvelling at the fragments. I pondered then that a book could be written.

I returned to my life in Australia and maintained periodic contact with Dr. Bell. Like the undertow that pulls waves back into the ocean, I felt pulled to keep in touch with Dr. Bell. So, while on vacation and exploring the world, I returned to visit her in New Delhi in 1999 and then again in Thailand in 2011.

A few years later, in November 2015, I visited Dr. Bell while I was attending a conference in Canada. One evening, as she told me stories of her life and adventures, I suggested she write her story. She indicated that others had similar ideas, but she simply responded, "My flare is more for talking than for writing." Dr. Bell would say that sometime during that week I offered to write her story, but as I remember it, she challenged me with "Why don't *you* write it?" Either way, it was the beginning.

Over the ensuing years, Dr. Bell graciously allowed me to sift through her life. I explored Dr. Bell's birthplace, the countryside familiar to her youth, and the place where her bones will rest. I wanted to familiarize myself with the sights, and sounds, and smells that Dr. Bell knew.

We travelled in the United States for two months, meeting family, friends, colleagues, and supporters. I interviewed and gathered material. We stepped into many different people's lives for a day, or maybe two, and I watched and listened as Dr. Bell's life unfolded from her interactions with others.

There was always delight in the meetings and loads of laughter in the sharing of memories. Sometimes there was a silent pause as a deep sadness or trouble was remembered. Each visit was like stepping into an old photograph, with Dr. Bell re-entering people's lives as if no time had passed.

Together, we spent a couple of days in the international office of her charity. We combed through old photographs, magazine articles, and the minutes of business meetings held in the United States, Canada, and India.

I joined Dr. Bell and her friends for a week's vacation in Wales, eager to take hold of the opportunity to spend time with two ladies who had worked alongside Dr. Bell in the early days in India.

PREFACE

When we travelled to Chicago, Illinois, to attend a weeklong conference, we discovered copies of her newsletters tucked away in a filing cabinet in the basement of Calvary Memorial Church, one of her supporting churches. Miraculously, the letters dating back to 1964 had survived a church fire in the 1970s.

One of the most remarkable sources of information was an old brown envelope crammed with handwritten letters from Dr. Bell to her sister Dorothy and brother-in-law Harry. It contained a letter written during Dr. Bell's voyage on a freighter ship from New York to Bombay[1] in 1964. Dr. Bell was twenty-seven years old.

Another invaluable source was the many hours Dr. Bell and I looked through hundreds of slides of her world adventures, beginning in Arabia in 1963. We borrowed an old slide projector, and Dr. Bell reminisced while I wrote copious notes.

As time passed, I also began to know some of Dr. Bell's nieces and nephews and their children; they shared memories and impressions of Dr. Bell and their family. I was also privileged to talk at length with her sister Sheila who recounted many stories of life on the farm.

Her adventures and travels have taken her to many places; she remembers at least forty-eight countries. It was impossible to recount every story. Even now as I write, I smile as I can hear Dr. Bell's voice recounting the earthquake she slept through in India, the time her sister Ruby took her shopping for a hat, her travels in

---

[1] Now called Mumbai.

Ladakh with Leela, and her affection for the Malto people, whose population was declining because of cerebral malaria, kala-azar disease, and tuberculosis. These moments will fade. But other tales have been preserved, for a time, in this book. I prayed that God would empty my pen and fill it with His ink. And He did (but that is a story for another time).

In preparing to write, I met with my high school teacher for advice. "Find Dr. Bell's voice," he told me. And so, I wrote Dr. Bell's biography as if she herself were penning her memoirs. As such, keep a Canadian twang in your ear as you read!

It is my prayer that Dr. Bell's story reflects the God we serve. The twelve chapters resonate with Joshua 4:4-7, where twelve stones collected from the riverbed stood as a memorial of God's faithfulness. With God, her story is a mosaic of miracles as she dedicated her life to defend the cause of the poor and needy.

When I left India in 1996 to return home to Australia, I embroidered the words of Jeremiah 22:16 on a piece of cloth for her: "He defended the cause of the poor and needy, and so all went well. Is that not what it means to know me?' declares the Lord."[2] Back then, and now, this small verse rings true in her life.

I asked Dr. Bell why she asked me to help her to write her story. She said, "Because you write from the heart—and I want my story not to glorify me but to glorify God." May this be so.

---

[2] Jeremiah 22:16 (NIV)

Aletta Grace Bell 1938

Honour your father and mother. Then you will live a long, full life in the land the Lord your God is giving you.

Exodus 20:12 (NLT)

FAMILY

He had done it at least a hundred times before, but this one time, my dad lost his grip on the outswing. When the stack of hay in the barn loft was low, he would climb the vertical ladder, wrap his hands around the horizontal beam, and propel himself into the haymow, where the hay was stored. On this occasion, Dad plunged at least twenty feet,[1] breaking his fall on the wooden floor below. When the black ambulance swallowed him up and drove him away, my six-year-old brain believed he had been taken away in a hearse; I thought Dad was dead. Struck with a stabbing pain in my stomach, I sobbed quietly in my bed.

Arriving home from school, Mother commented that Dad had not come in from the barn since lunch, where he had gone to feed the cattle. Alone in the barn and unable to move, my dad whistled and called Trixie to him. (Trixie was a free-range farm dog with little training, other than to come to the call of his name. He ran and played unrestrained.) Trixie ran up the gangway

---

[1] 6.1 meters

to my father's voice. Time after time, Trixie kept running out into the open yard and back up the gangway, but my mother did not notice his unusual frantic pattern and failed to see this distress signal from my dad.

It was my sister Sheila who found him when she walked into the barn to do her chores. She sounded the alarm, rushing back to the house to tell Mother. Mother telephoned for help. (We had a phone hanging on the wall with a hand crank that you wound around, signalling the operator to connect your call.)

It was a cold month, November. A light snow covered the ground, but not enough to stop a vehicle driving in. Dad had been lying there for hours in the cold. People said it was a miracle he did not get pneumonia. With his Scottish grit and humour, he always claimed that he had never taken any offence from the fall—it was the sudden stop that had assaulted him.

Hiding in the background as the people who came in the ambulance worked, I watched everything: a bone stuck out of his arm, his skin gaped open, and blood was all over the place. When they bent his arm up into a sling, he barely made a sound. He talked and seemed to joke and laugh with the people helping him. That was so Dad—he kept his humour in difficulty. I had a tight knot in my stomach; I knew he was badly hurt. He could not stand because his right leg would not hold him up. My eyes could not see what was wrong. Later, I discovered that he had broken his hip.

Dad was in hospital in London, Ontario, for what seemed like forever, and my brother Gordon was summoned home to Kincardine Township to take care of the manual labour on the farm. There were animals to feed and tend, and although Gordon loathed farming, he came home to help.

Two or three weeks after he arrived, Gordon came down with the measles. Mother was so fearful of catching them, she avoided going up the stairs to his room. My sister Dorothy took water and food to him. It was not long before he shared the virus with Dorothy, Sheila, and me. Gordon recovered and was back to working the farm. He would check on us when he came inside. Isolated upstairs, our bodies ached with fever, and my throat felt parched and sore. Gordon was a welcome sight with a fresh pitcher of water.

Even though Mother did not come upstairs, she was inevitably infected. Mother's sickness prompted her to send Dad a letter. (It was unlikely that Mother visited him in hospital, so communication was by letter.) She told him she was dying and she needed him home. He requested an early discharge from the hospital, arriving home wrapped in plaster casts. Boy, was I glad to see him! It was the first time since he had been taken away. (Children were forbidden visitors in a hospital, and besides, a bus ride to London, Ontario, was a full day's journey.)

Dad mended with a stiff arm. Putting pen to paper became problematic, so he taught himself to write with the other hand. Weakened by his injuries, even though his wounds had healed, the farm chores became physically challenging. Occasionally, I would stay home from school to help him harness the big horse, Jack. Unable to continue managing the farm without one of the boys, we became town dwellers when I approached adolescence.

Six years earlier, when his ninth child was born in the front room of the old farmhouse on Concession Road 10 in Kincardine Township, Dad, Daniel Bell, was fifty-three years old.[2] A late-season snowstorm in March 1937 brought the arrival of his youngest daughter—yours truly—Aletta Grace (pronounced Ah-LEE-tah). The local midwife came, caught me, and tied my cord.

Dad was older than Mother. They met when Mother worked in Dad's family home as a house cleaner. Dad grew up in a Scottish settlement in Kincardine Township, Bruce County, Canada. When my grandparents immigrated from the Isle of Tiree, Scotland, they brought the language of their homeland and shared it with their children. Although my dad grew up bilingual, his Gaelic tongue ended with the coming of the next generation; his Scottish voice was silenced.

Dad enjoyed sharing the pithy sayings he had learned. They were so well rehearsed and repeated, we thought he himself had penned them. Whatever their origin, his mottoes webbed in the corner of our minds and sometimes helped us through tough times.

---

[2] Historically, land in Ontario was divided into concessions and lots. Concession Roads were built between these strips to provide access to the parcels of land.

His intellect and sense of humour warmed people to him. A quiet, softly spoken man, Dad was kind and gentle and avoided open conflict. He never said too much when under fire from Mother. He kept peace whenever possible and covered his thoughts with a chuckle. Hardworking, he provided a subsistent livelihood for his family. During the Great Depression, Dad often reminisced, "You had potatoes and cabbage for lunch and cabbage and potatoes for supper." In that day, an ice cream at the fall fair cost five cents, a once a year indulgence. Dad told me, he once sold a pig for five dollars.

My dad supported his children, no matter what. In his quiet yet determined way, Dad stood for us. When my eldest sister, Lorelie, was three, her appendix burst. (Penicillin was not available in 1919: a person's body had to fight an infection; there were no such thing as antibiotics.) They summoned Dad into the operating room. Her prospects looked grim. She was more likely to die than to live.

"You might as well take it out while you're in there," he told them. They advised him that he could not stay in the hospital. "Well," he said, "I'm not leaving." A camp cot was set up, and Dad stayed. The nurses realized that he would not move from his daughter's side. He stayed by her side until she could come home. Lorelie survived and lived to the age of ninety-six.

By the time I began to explore ideas and form opinions about the world around me, my dad was well fixed in what he believed. When our attitudes on topics differed, we kept our closeness. I respected his thoughts and kept my own secure. I did not worry too much about our differences but enjoyed the debate. In the same way, Gordon and I often disputed age-old controversies.

Physical affection from either of my parents was unfamiliar to me. The first time my dad ever hugged me was when I departed for India at age twenty-seven. I knew that he would miss me. He embraced me and kissed my cheeks. Feeling his arms squeezed around my shoulders gave me a mixture of happiness and sadness. There was a sense of delight in the melancholy. I always knew my father's love. He encouraged and supported all my endeavours, no matter how crazy they seemed. He was my dad and I loved him.

Mother thought she was in "the menopause" when she discovered that she was carrying me. In 1973, on a road trip across Canada with some of my family, we visited relations out west. My sister Effie was making pancakes for breakfast when my cousin blurted out, "We know how old you are, Aletta, because your mom thought she was done having babies when you popped out!" That was news to me. I pondered this new fact that I was an unexpected arrival as Mother approached forty years of age. Perhaps that is why she never really bonded with me—what a shock it must have been to realize she was pregnant when she thought she had finished having babies!

Mother was known as Viola. When she applied for the old-age pension, she needed a copy of her birth certificate, where she discovered her name was in fact Violet! Mother was happiest as the centrepiece. If anybody else moved toward the limelight, her happiness faded. She crafted her own way of keeping the focus on herself. She was a stern woman, even to her grandchildren; nobody deliberately upset Grandma. She braided her hair and coiled it around on the top of her head. Her voice resonated, and she laughed loudly.

As matriarch, the family respected her despite her blinkered opinions set in stone. Family would dutifully write her letters, but inadvertently offend her. She often found insult in conversation, and people's actions rarely met her high moral standards. Mother broke relationship with others easily. Sometimes her silence announced her disapproval, and other times she clearly communicated her disdain.

She was almost ninety-three years old when she died. The news reached me in India by way of telegram. Saddened, but not bereft, I knew that Mother had joined Dad in Heaven.

My family, the Bell family, were strong, independent, and hardworking people. I have often credited the character of my family to our Scottish heritage, holding up the Bell family crest with pride. But we were also a product of our era. The Great Depression and world wars imprinted our lives. Poverty and fear sometimes encircled us, yet we were never hungry or in danger.

We had fresh milk from our cows, eggs from our chickens, and food from the fields. We squirrelled food in our basement for the winter, buried carrots in the dirt floor, and wrapped cabbages in newspaper.

Our lives were bound to the farm, with its list of chores; the church, with Sunday services at nearby Glammis Baptist; and the one-roomed elementary school, one mile from home and one mile back, on foot. Dad did not buy a car until he figured his family was complete. He always said he could not afford both. But then I came along, and he had to afford both the car and me.

There was no electricity on the farm. We had an outhouse (an outside toilet with no plumbing), a wash bowl in a stand in our bedroom, and a chamber pot for night-time tinkles. Winter was memorably cold with the inside of the bedroom windows frozen with ice, but to my young eyes, it looked like snow. The snowplow did not find its way along the 10th Concession, and the only way out was with horse and sleigh or a cutter.

Families memorialize events in the telling and retelling of them. All of what I know of my siblings as children is from old photographs and the stories that they have handed down to me. Listening to them as a child, I absorbed them into my own memories. When I retell them, it is as if I were there, but looking back, I know that I wasn't. Although my older siblings had mostly left home before I was born, our not growing up together did not weaken our bond. I grew into my family, learning far more about them as we aged.

We were like three families rolled into one. The three oldest were Lorelie, Milton, and Effie. The next bundle were Ruby, Archie, and Gordon. Followed by Dorothy, Sheila, and me. Of all my siblings, I only really remember Gordon, Sheila, and Dorothy being at home on the farm.

Although my sister Ruby left home well before I was born, the fifteen-year gap between us made her more like a mother to me than a sister. She was the daughter whom Mother always called upon when she needed help at home—and if Mother called, you answered. In my early childhood, "Booby" was all that I could make of the name Ruby (not that I truly remember, but that is what my family recounted). As an infant in our family photograph, I sit contentedly on Ruby's knee under the watchful eye of Lorelie. It was Ruby who mothered me through my awkward teenage years. So, when I earned a place in medical school, Ruby was who I ran to, to tell the news. I can still remember bounding up the stairs; my heart was about to burst with the excitement.

Lorelie, my eldest sister, also mothered me with kindness when she came home to visit. She always called me Aletta Grace and would snuggle me into her lap. She had moved out west, and her two girls were born only eleven months apart. (In India, women thought that while they were breastfeeding a baby, they could not get pregnant. I would tell them, "Do not believe that myth. My older sister has two daughters, and for one month of the year, they are both the same age!")

Lorelie would take me shopping when I was home on leave. One time she bought me a stylish, candy-red blouse, a soft silky synthetic with ruffles trimming the front and the sleeves. Her gift to me was a generous offering from her limited resources; I will always cherish and keep it. In the time we had together, Lorelie and I forged a warm sisterly bond.

I was the little one, and my siblings spoiled me. Sheila, the next one up from me, was glad when I was born: she was not the baby anymore. It became her job to rock me to sleep in the baby carriage. When she saw my eyes close and that all was quiet, she would stop. To her dismay, the instant I lost momentum, my eyes would fly open! Annoyingly, she could not go out and play until she got me to sleep.

As a small child, I slept on a straw-tick mattress that was hard and lumpy. The straw that kept me dry was replaced once a year in the springtime. As soon as I was able to get up at night to pee in the pot, I was allowed to sleep on a proper mattress. Being the youngest carried the advantage of being first in the bathtub! Mother would fill the tub behind the woodstove once a week on a Saturday to clean us all up for church on Sunday.

Effie was my fun sister. She was sunny natured, not easily ruffled, and ever resourceful. At age three, I was her flower girl when she married Bob, but I have no recollection of the event. The wedding was at the farm.

She was the first in the family to marry and the first to move away from Mother. Later in life, Mother moved in to live with Effie for a time, and when I was home, I would stay with them occasionally.

Milton, my oldest brother, served in the army. When Dad was recuperating after his fall, Milton also came home to help. Contented in the barn, Milton was my ally in Dad's absence. He was a gentle tease—in our family, mocking each other was an expression of love. One evening he looked at me, his face as stern as he could make it, and said, "Tomorrow you need to have those horses up from the field, harnessed, and ready for work." He had a twinkle in his eye, but I was not certain. Sincere or not, he did not think I could do it. Next morning, I climbed out of bed at daybreak. He was surprised and proud, exclaiming, "I didn't really think you would do it!" One of my favourite exchanges with Milton was when I would stand up tall, clench my fists, and show him my muscles. "Yep, just like chicken legs," he would say. And we would laugh together.

My middle brother, Archie, was in the air force and off at war. Whenever he came home, he always brought chocolates or some other luxury. Sadly, I never really had the opportunity to know him. He married—and later died—during my first stint in India. Initially misdiagnosed with a bad case of indigestion, he collapsed and died: it was his heart. He was forty-three years old.

In the midst of absorbing the lives and memories of my siblings, I created a few of my own. In the summer of 1948, I was eleven and my family was hosting two weddings on the farm. Eleven is a critical age for a girl. It was the night before one of the weddings, and Lorelie was late in arriving home. Mother said I had to go to bed. "I can't go to bed until Lorelie comes home to do my hair," I protested. Mother was unrelenting and insisted. In a fountain of tears, I obeyed. When Lorelie finally reached home, she crept quietly upstairs and rolled my hair in rags. Next morning, with ringlets bouncing around my face, my tears evaporated into smiles.

Although, a spoiled child, I knew how to work. I could wield a hay fork and spread-out sheaves of hay. Granted, when I first started imitating Dad, the hay fork impaled my foot! In the winter, I milked the cow, aiming the occasional squirt toward the kittens. Being in the barn with Dad was the best place. Sometimes I helped Dad by walking the horse down the gangway, harnessed to ropes and a pulley to haul bundles of hay up into the mow. There was no saddle. One time I was waiting for Dad, sitting bareback with a hand on the reins. The horse bent down for a nibble, and I slid neatly down his neck! Sitting face-to-face with my equine friend, he did not flinch a muscle; he just kept munching on his grassy snack.

My first memory of chocolate was Ex-Lax, a chocolate laxative or "purgative," as Mother would say. I was always extremely careful when I stole anything, taking only one piece. I was skilled at stealing sweet things from the pantry. My sweet tooth easily succumbed (and still does) to the presence of treats—even those reserved for guests and declared off limits by Mother. Admittedly, I was adept at telling lies to keep myself out of trouble. Anyhow, one Ex-Lax was all it took! The next day, I was frequenting the outhouse—Mother never did figure out why.

There were other things hidden from Mother. With my Scottish roots, porridge was a staple for breakfast. Despite adding fresh milk and oodles of sugar, I just could not swallow it! My furry friend, Trixie, kept my secret. Surreptitiously, every morning, I tipped my bowl outside under a bush, and Trixie hid the evidence in his belly!

Then there was the time one of the cows stood on my bare foot. When its hoof pressed into my big toe, I remembered Mother's instruction, "Don't go into the barn in bare feet." Simple, right? Except, I was not always particularly good at doing what I was *supposed* to do. I paced the floor to ease the throbbing pain, but I could not tell anybody because I was not supposed to be in there without shoes.

Even though I had eight older siblings, the age gap, and the resulting life gap, made me more like an only child. With nobody near my age to play with, the animals on the farm became my company: the horses, the kittens, the calves, the chickens, and my dog, Trixie. Trixie was born around the same time as I was. My siblings told me that a neighbour's dog had a litter of puppies, Heinz variety, and they had no use for them. Trixie was one of those puppies. We grew up together, and he became my best friend. When I was small, he would pull me along in the sleigh. When I grew too heavy for Trixie, the winter calf (born and raised in the winter cold) would pull me along.

Childhood collided with the fire and brimstone of Mother. She had an unpredictable list of rules. I did not deliberately disobey Mother, but it was not too difficult to upset her, so I often escaped to the barn, the animals, or the back forty. The back forty was an area of bushland adjacent to our farm. It belonged to somebody else, and in the summertime produced a feast of wild raspberries and apples. When Mother could not find me, Dad knew where I was.

My solitary way of life made me shy and introverted. My shyness sometimes overwhelmed me, and as a small child, I would stick my finger in my mouth; even though teased by those close to me, sucking it gave me comfort. Sometimes I felt different, like I did not really fit. I always wanted to go in bare feet, and I did not like dolls, as girls were supposed to. I understood animals better than I could figure out most people.

I discovered the joy of Christmas in childhood. My siblings always came home, and I am sure they came bearing gifts just for me. It was a momentous time. Even when my siblings were married, they came back for Christmas Day. In elementary school, we put on a cracker of a concert. We learned verses and carols, and our teacher helped us to learn monologues and rehearse our parts in the plays. When I lived abroad, one of the delights of coming home to Canada was celebrating Christmas with my family. The fresh falling and blowing snow were a welcome change from the dusty heat of India.

My older siblings had a very tough existence in their formative years, and they did not have the opportunity to attend high school as I did. They were all intensely proud of their baby sister and, to their credit, harboured no bitterness or resentment toward me. My brothers could have been jealous, but they were amazing as they never seemed envious of my education and opportunities. All of them were good to me. They celebrated my achievements with me and supported me, like a huge net stretched beneath a trapeze.

During medical school, my sister Dorothy spared me from homelessness. She was living in one room in an upstairs flat in London, Ontario, and I was living in one room on the eighth floor at Victoria Hospital, where interns resided to meet the demands of being on call overnight. Feeling unwell with fever, I took myself to the health clinic at University Hospital. A shot of penicillin in the butt was the standard treatment. The next day, feeling no better and noticing a tiny spot on my wrist, I returned for another consultation. Usually, I walked between the hospitals, but by this time, I was feeling too sick to step far, so I took the bus. When the doctor poked his nose into the waiting room, seeing me there, he said, "You better call that one in—looks like a bus ran over her!"

He confirmed that I had chicken pox and placed me under quarantine for one month. Aside from the cleaning lady, who came into my room daily to wash the floor, nobody else would disturb me. However, she noticed my rash and reported my illness, and so I had to leave my lodging to isolate myself from the other interns. The hospital offered to accommodate me in the infectious ward, an open room with beds side-by-side and a communal bathroom at one end. I telephoned Dorothy and told her my predicament. She took me in. She had one bed and a couch.

Effie was the only sibling to visit me in India. When Effie came in December 1987, we had a fantastic time together! She tagged along with her daughter Marabelle, who had her own itinerary. Effie and I spent one month together, sightseeing on all modes of travel I could expose her to. We travelled by train in first class AC (air-conditioning), second class AC, second class non-AC (no air-conditioning!), but I spared her third class (that we, the expats, refer to as "cattle class"). Effie delighted in our journeys by way of auto rickshaw, a small three-wheeled vehicle powered by a motorcycle engine; cycle rickshaw; एक्का (*ekka*), a light two-wheeled horse-driven passenger cart; bullock cart; and bus. She only had a little difficulty navigating the steps of the bus on the upward thrust—not too bad for a sixty-nine-year-old lady!

The two of us explored Jaipur, in Rajasthan, and the Nilgiris district, in the southern hills of Tamil Nadu. In Rajasthan, we watched the watering of the fields using a Persian wheel driven by two camels: the wheel and buckets circled round and round and round, drawing water from its source and channelling it out onto the land.

We stayed with Indian friends in Calcutta[3] who worked there with the poor. They helped Effie to satisfy her greatest wish in coming to India: to shake Mother Teresa's hand. The Mother House of the Missionaries of Charity was home to Mother Teresa. If she was home, she welcomed guests. My friends telephoned and found her to be home that day, so they took both of us there. Effie and I visited with her, and we shook her hand. She gave each of us a card. It held her wisdom of the Five Fruits of Silence:

>The fruit of SILENCE is Prayer
>The fruit of PRAYER is Faith
>The fruit of FAITH is Love
>The fruit of LOVE is Service
>The fruit of SERVICE is Peace

She spoke with us in English. Overcome with delight, Effie thanked Mother Teresa profusely. I thanked her too. It was like shaking hands with anybody, except she was not just anybody—she was Mother Teresa. She was a little, old, hunched-over lady; a beautiful lady with a

---

[3] Now known as Kolkata.

beautiful smile. Her eyes were compassionate and reflected love.

Years later, when I was home on break from India, my family listened with fascination to my adventures and watched slideshows in their living rooms. One of my nieces only recognized me as the owner of the inky handwriting inside the blue-coloured aerograms.

One time, I came home to Canada for surgery. I had a very large abdominal mass and wondered if I would ever be able to return to India. Thankfully, it revealed itself to be a benign uterine fibroid (as big as a melon). I was anemic, exhausted, and malnourished from my work in India. Gordon and his wife, Anne, provided a home base for me: a place to heal and restore. I relished in Anne's home cooking and enjoyed sharing meals around the table with their two daughters. Having come from village life in India where I wore only traditional clothing, I needed clothes. Gordon and Anne provided for me, sending their daughters to help me choose what was fashionable at that time.

My oldest brother, Milton, always welcomed my arrival home to Canada with a car. He was the car guy: the first in the family to own one. Aside from being mechanically sound, the car he prepared for me always had tires with ample tread and dependable brakes. He understood his sister's need for speed!

All my family brought their individual skills to the table in their care of me. When I graduated from medical school, they arranged a party for me at Gordon and Anne's house. They pooled their resources to give me a three-piece luggage set, a blue ensemble of Samsonite. As I transitioned from my permanent residence in India to a life mostly back in Canada, Ruby telephoned me often, calling in the evenings to make sure I had eaten supper. My brothers and my sisters watched over me, even as my hair greyed.

My life journey took me far away from my family, and yet, it brought me closer to them. The distance, periods of long absence, and infrequent visits home kept us together in a unique way. Family is the first memorial stone of God's grace in my life; the first stone collected from a lifetime of memories. My family's embrace and unconditional love reflect a glimpse of God's devotion toward me, reminding me of His faithfulness. Without Him—and without them—I could not have accomplished the good things He had planned for me to do. My family's love helped me to understand the love and the grace of my Heavenly Father, and to achieve far more than I could ever have imagined.

FAMILY

Back Row: Lorelie, Milton, Effie, Archie
Middle Row: Gordon, Daniel (Dad), Sheila, Ruby, Dorothy, Violet (Mother)
Front Row: Aletta

Family Farm
Aletta's birthplace

"Wedding Curls"
1940 Effie & Bob's wedding at family farm
Back Row: Bob, Effie
Front Row: Aletta Grace, flower girl

You have been taught the holy Scriptures from childhood, and they have given you the wisdom to receive the salvation that comes by trusting in Christ Jesus.

2 Timothy 3:15 (NLT)

FAITH

I sat beside him on the three-legged stool we used for milking the cows. My dog, Trixie, lay stretched out on his side, panting, his tail limp. I scooped water from the cattle trough, and he took a little from my hand. I stroked him and rested my hand softly on his neck; his eyes were glazed open and sad, his ears crinkled back on his head. Mother had wrapped a mustard plaster around his middle, and I winced inside, remembering the burn of a poultice that had once swathed my ribcage. Trixie, sick with pneumonia, had jumped over the half door and escaped Mother's first treatment bandage.

The exposure to the outside had made him deathly ill as his weakened chest was crushed by the ice-cold air. Mother said he had double pneumonia. There was no money to call for a veterinarian. I prayed for him to recover, but he weakened every day. His nose was wet and sticky, and he struggled to breathe.

I cannot remember my exact words, but I made a bargain with God. It was a simple, child-like trust when I gave my word to God. I promised that if He saved Trixie, I would do whatever He asked me to do. When Trixie lifted his head, I knew that he would pull through.

He recovered; my much-loved companion bounded back to health. It was the beginning of the greatest change in my life.

Every Sunday morning, I joined the flock at Glammis Baptist Church. It was a country gathering, founded in 1874 when a group of twelve people met together with a reverend from nearby Tiverton, Ontario. In its early days, Glammis Baptist supervised the behaviour of its members and defended a rigid code of conduct. Mother, steeped in religion, was always eager to modify our behaviour; her interpretation of godliness governed by an ever-growing list of rules.

In the horse-and-buggy days, church life was akin to farming life. My brothers and sisters sometimes reminisced about the five-mile[1] walk from the farm to the church. They remembered that it was a long walk there—and a longer walk home. Their feet throbbed, squished into their Sunday shoes. Dad always had horses, so I am sure that the walks to and from church were less frequent than my siblings recall, especially in the wintertime with snow-covered fields and unplowed roads; they would not have made the journey on foot. My recollection was that Dad drove us in his 1930s Studebaker. I was thankful that he had decided that he could afford both me *and* the car!

---

[1] eight kilometres

Glammis Baptist was a sturdy church, built with a steep triangular roof. Inside, smooth wooden pews lined up row by row, leading to a lectern, raised platform and small baptistery.[2] My family filled two pews, and we were known as the "Bells and all the little Bells," but that was probably before I came along. The front lancet-shaped doors and coordinating window frames identified the building as a place where Christians gathered. Specimen vases, supporting a single-stemmed artificial flower, sat inside each frosted window. A decorative chandelier was firmly suspended in the centre of the room.

The organ and the choir fostered my enjoyment of music and the hymns of old. The church held classes on Sundays to teach children Bible stories. My Sunday school teacher, Mrs. Groves, was a kind and gentle lady who introduced me to the song, "This Little Light of Mine." Delighted with its melody, I sang that song repeatedly, so they say. It is a tune that has travelled with me for over eighty years.

My teacher talked about Jesus and about His life. Although I grew up in a home that espoused God, His nearness seemed extremely far away. From very young, I remember observing the contradictions of religion, and on occasion, I was the recipient of its injustice.

Early in my childhood, without knowing exactly why, I firmly decided that I did not want to be baptised in

---

[2] A sunken receptacle used for baptism by total immersion.

the confines of a church tradition. Perhaps because I knew that I could never measure up to what was expected. However, Mrs. Groves was different, and she began to show me the heart of God. She introduced me to the sacred writings of God as lived and penned through His followers. She helped me to know Him by teaching His Word, the Bible. I discovered God was a loving God. He somehow wove a thread of His love into the core of me. He was near to me, protecting me, rather than being a distant, far-off overseer of rules in the sky. God cared for me.

At eight years old, having grown up with the Second World War, I had not experienced a world at peace. My two older brothers, Milton and Archie, served in the army and air force, respectively. They were men away at war, and I did not see them. The war ended, and the world suddenly changed. And for whatever reason, I thought that the end of the world was coming. I cannot explain why I thought that as a child, but I did, and I was afraid of going to Hell.

In my early years, I understood that Hell was a place filled with fire and brimstone, where dead sinners departed to. Not that I knew much about brimstone, but I had the impression that it was bad, *really* bad. Mother reminded me every other day that I was going there if I did not repent of my sins. I had figured out that a sin was any infraction of Mother's rules, but I was not too sure about what I had to do to repent!

Sundays were not exactly fun days, restricted to church-only activities. Sometimes I would sneak out to the barn to play with the kittens. I would pick them up and take them with me into the horses' feeding box. The deep wooden trough filled with hay concealed our play, and no one disturbed me hidden away in there.

Sunday afternoons, we listened to the *Old Fashioned Revival Hour*, a radio broadcast created by Charles E. Fuller. Toward the end of each program, Charles invited listeners to make a pledge to follow Jesus. With my juvenile imaginings of the imminent end of the world, Kincardine Township could soon fall into the Great Lakes, and I was not ready to burn in Hell. Under the guidance of Charles' voice, I knelt in front of the radio and told God how sorry I was for being such a rotten, naughty girl. It was my first step toward Him. I asked God to forgive me and to accept me into His family. Heaven-bound, I was ready for the end of the world.

There was nothing private about my confession that Sunday, and Mother began to agitate about baptism. In those days, they had tent meetings. Large tents were set up for community gatherings, and everyone was welcome. People came together to listen to a preacher. It was a way to tell people about Jesus in a public arena. The Baptist churches in the area held meetings, but being on an independent site meant that they were not exclusively Baptist, so anybody could come. I responded well to this universal program because I would not be baptised into a church tradition, but rather, I would be baptised as in the days of the Bible: out in the open, announcing faith in the living

God, acknowledging His son, Jesus, and being filled with His Spirit.

A tent meeting had been set up near the Saugeen River, just outside of Chesley, Ontario, where my sister Effie lived. In the summer while visiting Effie, I met my friend Faith. We were about the same age, and her dad was a pastor. He was baptising people at the end of the meetings. Alongside Faith and her sister, I waded into the Saugeen River and presented myself. One by one, Faith's dad gently pushed us under the water and baptised us in the name of the Father, the Son, and the Holy Spirit. As he pulled my face out of the water, I gulped the air and wiped the water from my eyes. Not letting go of my hand, he guided me back to the riverbank. My life did not change very much, but Mother was happy because she thought it was time.

Someone influential to my faith was Elizabeth, a schoolteacher who worked in Igbaja, Nigeria, for thirty-eight years. She would give talks at Glammis Baptist when she was home on leave. She spoke about her life and her vocation in West Africa. Her retelling of Bible stories resonated within me, and the music of her life stirred up a sense of awareness in mine.

Elizabeth related stories from the Bible to help illustrate the motivation for her work. Listening to her as a child, I embraced her message. She taught the words of Scripture through the actions of her life. At age ten or eleven, I wanted to be like Elizabeth, travelling to a faraway land where the sun blazed and the people spoke a different language. I wanted to do the work the Lord had planned and designed for me.

My earlier childhood promise to God came back into my mind. He had accomplished His end of the bargain and saved Trixie. Was this what He was asking me to do?

One Bible story Elizabeth told that influenced me as a child was a story from the Old Testament[3] of four leprosy sufferers who were sitting outside the city gates of the Jewish city of Samaria.[4] Enemies of the Jews, the Arameans, had set up camp outside Samaria and trapped God's people inside the walled city. The four leprosy sufferers were starving, and with famine inside the city, they decided to surrender themselves to the Arameans. They knew the Arameans might kill them, but they would die anyway if they stayed at the city gate.

When they came to the edge of the Aramean camp, no one was there! Unbeknownst to them, the Lord had caused the Aramean army to flee their camp in the night. Excitedly, the four men gorged themselves and gathered silver, gold, and clothing, carefully hiding their hoard. Soon, the men realized that this was not right. It was a day of good news, and they were not sharing it with anyone. They went back and shared the good news with the people inside the city.

---

[3] The Old Testament, the first portion of the Bible, contains the sacred scriptures of the Jewish people.
[4] 2 Kings 7:3–9

Elizabeth's retelling of this ancient account helped me to realize that I had *Good News* about how Jesus made it possible for me to live with God forever. I could stay at home in Canada and feast on the Good News, or I could take the knowledge of this great treasure with me to people in far-off places who were suffering inside their cities, waiting for someone to share the Good News with them.

Another story Elizabeth told that shaped my thinking and helped develop my compassion for others was the narrative of Jesus feeding five thousand men and their families.[5] In this story, a huge crowd of people greeted Jesus just as he arrived in a remote area. Even though Jesus wanted to be alone, because He had recently received news that His relative John had died in prison, Jesus had compassion on the crowd of people and healed their sick.

At the end of the day, Jesus did not want to send the crowd home hungry, so He asked His disciples to feed them. But the disciples protested, saying they did not have enough to give them. Unperturbed, Jesus asked them to bring him what they had. Between them, they presented five loaves of bread and two fish. Jesus asked the disciples to have the people sit down in groups. He thanked His Father in Heaven and blessed the meal. Breaking the bread into pieces, He handed it to His disciples to give out to the crowd of people. Amazingly, everybody ate as much as they wanted, and the disciples picked up twelve baskets of leftovers!

---

[5] Matthew 14:13-21

The emphasis I embraced as a child was that *all* the people ate their fill. Jesus fed *everybody* with what the disciples had given Him. A meal that the disciples thought insufficient, Jesus transformed into abundantly more than enough. Elizabeth likened the groups to represent all the different peoples in the world. She encouraged us to realize that the Good News about Jesus is for *everybody*. As steadfast followers of Jesus, we too could give what we possessed to share with others. Jesus could bless what we gave and could do far more than we could ever hope or imagine. The Lord used these two stories to speak to my heart and mind.

Moving through my teenage years toward adulthood, my faith was unknowingly nurtured in the company of my high school friends. Farm kids tended to gravitate toward each other and stick together. In those days, the 1950s, our parents heavily influenced our social life as they presided over our time spent with others. My high school friends' lives were like mine—we shared the commonality of belonging to church-going families, and church meant something to us. It was natural to talk about God.

When my family lived on the farm on the 10th Concession, my high school friend Shirley was a nearby neighbour. One winter morning, after my family had moved into nearby Tiverton, Shirley's dad slid into a ditch driving her to school. We invited Shirley to board with us for the winter so that she could attend high school with me. Our friendship cemented through those cold months as we shared my room and my bed. We shared our lives and our faith, forging a lifelong friendship.

In my experience, small independent churches to large globally-recognized denominations sometimes separate God's people from each other. We each interpret and speculate the true meaning of what is written and recorded in the Bible—sometimes we disagree, and sometimes our disagreement divides us. But there are mysteries in the Christian faith: unknown answers, unanswerable questions. Faith is believing in God, whom we cannot see, but being absolutely sure that He is there.[6]

The essence of my faith has always been belief in Jesus, God's son. Jesus is "the way, the truth, and the life. No one can come to the Father except through [Him]."[7] With a heritage steeped in religious conviction and a lengthy list of impossible-to-follow rules, God's Holy Spirit has led me on a lifelong journey toward understanding and accepting His grace and His deep, unfailing, and unfathomable love for me. God Himself loves me excessively, unjustifiably, and undeservedly. Jesus taught that we should love God with all our heart, soul, mind, and strength and that we should love others as we love ourselves.[8] This is the core of my faith.

---

[6] Hebrews 11:1 (GNT)
[7] John 14:6 (NLT)
[8] Mark 12:30–31 (CEV)

The promise I made to God that I would do whatever He asked if He saved Trixie changed me forever. I had no inspiration—or notion—to follow Jesus anywhere. God healing Trixie softened my heart toward Him. Before that, I only understood Him to be a distant authority who watched and judged my every move. But the Lord revealed His grace to me. He showed me that He did not come to judge me, but rather, He came to save me. He loves me more than I can understand or fully comprehend. He gave me the gift of faith.

Faith is the second memorial stone of God's grace in my life that He carved from before the beginning of time itself. Believing in Him, I have come to know Him. I aspired to keep a childhood promise to the Creator of the universe. Open to Him guiding my steps, He stretched me far beyond my youthful imaginings and the worldly constraints of poverty and gender. In the wise words of my high school friend Shirley, "As life develops, then you find out where God wants you to be."

Aletta & Trixie

Aletta reading from her Bible

Now all glory to God, who is able, through his mighty power at work within us, to accomplish infinitely more than we might ask or think.

                                        Ephesians 3:20 (NLT)

FOUNDATION

It is difficult to imagine now, but on my first day at school, I was scared spitless! Seated at my desk, wondering what to do, I fiddled with the inkwell in front of me. I flipped the metal lid up-down, down-up, up-down. . . My rhythm was suddenly broken by the teacher's voice. "What are you doing?" she demanded.

"Nothing," I mouthed softly.

"Liar!" she boomed, "You can stay in at recess for telling a lie." Innocent, I sat quietly and obeyed.

Not too long after lunch, I needed to pee (really badly), but with the injustice of the morning looming, I was too scared to raise my hand and ask permission to go. At the end of the day, I sprinted home to the safety of the back forty, leaving a small puddle in the classroom behind me. Trixie welcomed me home and bounded into the bush with me, tail wagging and barking with delight.

Unfortunately for me, my teacher boarded with my family that year. She told Mother of my wayward deed, and I was offered no opportunity to make my plea. Without inquiry, I was punished.

My learning began in a one-room country school with that one teacher, a religiously zealous woman. Her methods stretched back to a 15th century proverb that announced, "Children [in particular young women] should be seen and not heard." She kept close command on all the children from class 1 through to class 8. My siblings had prepared me for school days, pulling my chain with threats like, "You just wait until you get to school!" So, it was with apprehension that I approached. That teacher continued to prey on my fear.

One day, she called me to the front of the class and asked me to read out loud. But terror squeezed my throat, and I couldn't speak; not one word came out. Incensed, she shouted, "When you can open your mouth, you go ahead and read!" She left me standing there on display while she continued the lessons with the older children. The greatest lesson she taught me was the vulnerability of a child and what it felt like to have a voice that you couldn't use.

Miss Urquhart rescued me and my education the following year. She seemed to understand me and recognized my potential. Like a mother goose, she stretched out her wings and sheltered her students. From that safe place, she encouraged our learning and never asked us to do anything more than she knew we could. Egypt School,[1] as it was known, became a secure place for me where I was contented and happy to learn.

My oldest sister, Lorelie, was very clever, and she finished class 8 by age eleven—essentially, two years ahead of the school program. She was brilliant. Sadly, her ambition to become a teacher or a nurse was held back by our family's poverty. By age twelve, Lorelie was forced out of school to work. The same fate awaited some of my other siblings; education and a profession were nothing more than a fanciful hope for the older ones.

Living on the farm in Kincardine Township limited my scope. With elementary school being the highest level of education attained in my family, I wondered how I could become a schoolteacher like Elizabeth (the lady who stayed with us when she was home from her work and adventures in Nigeria). A feeling deep down motivated me as I contemplated working in a foreign land. Approaching adolescence, I talked to God about my need for more schooling, and I prayed that He would give me the opportunity to go to high school.

In those times, there were three things that a girl could aspire to. You could become a teacher, a nurse, or a clerical worker. Teachers, nurses, and secretaries learned their trade while working; there were no

---

[1] The 10th Concession of Kincardine Township was divided into an upper and lower section. The upper section school was named Egypt School, and the lower section school was named Canaan School. In the middle ran a creek known as the Red Sea. In those days, there was a one-roomed school every mile or so, enabling children living on farms access to elementary education on foot.

university courses to teach you. Essentially, you were an apprentice, and your teachers were more experienced senior staff. You learned as you worked! You didn't aim for any other professions because higher education was generally not considered a pursuit for girls. For most young women, marriage was their vocation. Having filled my childhood with animals, tree climbing, and walking barefoot outdoors, the idea of growing up to be a secretary, stuffed inside an office, held no appeal. As for becoming a nurse, all I knew about nurses was that they emptied bed pans—and that seemed disgusting. That left only one option: teaching.

Although high school was no more than three miles[2] down the road in Tiverton, it was a continuation school and offered only the lower-grade classes. The nearest high school where I could complete grade 13, the final year of secondary education, was Kincardine District High School (KDHS), eleven miles[3] from home. The same year I was ready to start high school, Mr. Thornicroft, the school principal of KDHS, announced that he was extending the bus route to include the 10th Concession, as the service was gearing up to collect students from the rural areas. But Dad laughed and asked him, "How will you get a bus down the 10th Concession in the wintertime? The snowplow only just clears a path wide enough for a horse and sleigh!"

Despite the obstacles, Dad and Mother decided to allow me to continue my education, an answer to prayer

---

[2] five kilometres
[3] eighteen kilometres

and deep longing. The school year began in September, and Dad drove me to and from Tiverton for the first week, having decided that the school bus to Kincardine would never make it through to the farm in the snowy months. Nonetheless, the following week, watching the Kincardine-bound bus drive right past where we lived, my ever-practical Dad helped me onboard. So began my first year at KDHS, one week late. I gazed out the window, the lush summer green was fading, and the briskness of fall was coming. With the change of season, I was stepping out of the farm and into the future.

In the meantime, Dad tried to persuade one of his sons to buy our family farm. But neither Archie nor Gordon showed interest, and although Milton held some sentiment, he was well situated in his job with General Motors. So, before the first snow, Dad sold the farm to outsiders and bought a house in Tiverton. From our new place, I would walk up to one of the stores to wait for the KDHS school bus. On bad stormy days, our bus driver blinked his lights and stuck his head out the window for a better look at the road ahead. He mostly made it through, but the buses travelling out to the farms never did.

By the time I reached high school, I had gained a modest confidence, and I discovered the teachers to be mostly fair-minded and wise. Keen to study, I became an avid reader and attained high marks. Public speaking was part of the curriculum, and I managed that quite well.

Starting one week into the school term, the best seats in the classroom were taken. As I stepped into the room, the teacher directed me to the desk smack bang in the middle of the front row. Surreptitiously, in between classes when nobody else was in the classroom, I broke my seat, determined to have myself removed from the front row. (The desk and seat were joined together and attached to the floor.) Thankfully, I was moved back a few rows to the next available desk, directly behind Catherine, the Anglican minister's daughter. From there, I was safely out of sight of one of our less agreeable teachers who picked on front row students. Catherine was top of the class until I tied for first. She was shy (like me), and I had the feeling that she was pressured to excel. Over time, we became friends. Walking past her desk, I would pull her hair tie, unravelling the bow, teasing her as a gesture of our friendship.

Not able to see the blackboard, I copied my notes from her work. I had petitioned Mother many times, telling her of my struggle. But she dismissed my claim because, in her opinion, there was nothing the matter with anybody's eyes in our family.

In class 12, we attended a guidance class to help us decide our future paths. As I remember, the teacher assessed our abilities (evaluating our strengths and weaknesses) and helped us to explore the possibilities. Given that I had already chosen teaching out of the three customary careers for women, there was opportunity to investigate the occupation in greater depth.

In a one-room country school, like the one I had attended, I was given the assignment of observing the teacher at work for a day. While seated at the rear of the room, always enthusiastic and eager to learn, I watched the classroom antics unfold. Two class 8 students were called up to the blackboard to work on a problem. Neither one could give an answer, and neither one seemed to want to *find* an answer. Their disinterest in learning appalled me. I could not understand why they neglected their opportunity to learn.

An indignation swirled in my gut, and I had the urge to bang their heads together. In that moment, at the age of seventeen, I realized I did not possess the disposition to teach unwilling young minds. I was devastated to realize that I couldn't possibly be a teacher. My world spiralled and landed with a thud! Forced to re-examine my aptitude for work, I decided in favour of becoming a nurse—bedpans surprisingly seemed more manageable.

One day our French teacher asked the class, "How many of you are going to university?" A few classmates raised their hands in response, but not me. University was well beyond my reach and expectation. Attending high school had already fulfilled my dreams. But the teacher looked at me and questioned, "*You* aren't going to university?" The tone in her voice betrayed her bewilderment.

I carried the privilege of high school as a great responsibility. I needed to do well for my family because I had the opportunity they had lacked. Determined and striving, I was a high-achieving student and ranked top of my class. Even so, university had never entered my thoughts—besides, my parents didn't have the means to send me. And so, I simply replied, "No."

Several weeks later, a university prospectus appeared on my desk. Without money, university was a pipe dream, and so, without ambition, I half-heartedly flipped through the brochure. But the next day, and the day after that, a different prospectus greeted me. Curiosity sprouted, and I began to explore and dream. If I could go to university, the only study that interested me was to become a doctor of medicine. There was no precedent; nobody in my family line had been a doctor. Looking back, who else but the Lord could have propagated such a thought? Without my knowing, He was guiding my steps.

As new ideas are cultivated, weeds can sprout and growth can be thwarted. Just the thought of moving to a big city daunted me, a timid country girl. But as I entertained the possibility, the hope of attending university emerged, I reasoned that one of the universities was in London, Ontario, where two of my siblings then resided. With my brother Gordon and my sister Dorothy living in London, I would not be alone. I was also somewhat familiar with the city, as the previous two summers I had stayed with Dorothy and worked a summer job as a housemaid.

When I looked at the entrance requirements for Western University, I discovered I needed three strands of mathematics, and I had taken only two. Mathematics was not my strongest subject, and I had avoided taking algebra. Disappointed, but not defeated, I sought advice from my principal, Mr. Thornicroft. I explained my dilemma, and he opened the big ledger on his desk to scrutinize my record. Eventually, he looked up and said, "Well, your marks in math are okay."

"But I don't like math," I interrupted, "we are part way through the year, and it would be hard for me to pick it up now. I don't really want to do another math."

He continued, "I understand that Western University will be changing the entry requirement this year. You will only need the two maths, and you have more than sufficient credits to apply for the premedical course."

Excitement budded, and so I asked, "Sir, could somebody without any money— and whose parents didn't have any money—could they go to medical school?" It was obvious that I was referring to myself. I held my breath and could hear my heart beating in my ears.

"With the help of government grants and scholarships, it is certainly possible!" he assured me. Excitement erupted, and in that moment, the idea of going to university became possible and ignited my desire to go. Brimming with anticipation, I told my parents that evening, expecting them both to share my enthusiasm. But to my shock and dismay, Mother just about hit the roof!

"No child of mine is ever going to university—that's the place of the devil!" She almost choked on her supper. Crestfallen, I retreated to the safety of silence and never mentioned it to Mother again.

Mother came from a different era, and both she and Dad were formally educated only as far as class 3. In Mother's opinion, university would introduce my young, vulnerable mind to teachings and ideas that were contrary to her beliefs and lure me into evil ways of thinking and behaving.

By way of prayer, I placed my problem before the Lord. It was a defining moment for me, deciding to go to university. The idea was fresh and enlivened me. Even though my mother objected, and I wasn't exactly sure if I would be able to finance medical school, I felt determined to pursue it. I deduced that if I had enough money for the first year, I would go. So, to be sure of the Lord's guiding—if He really wanted me to become a doctor—I asked Him to provide enough money to cover the expenses of the first year. Decidedly, if I didn't receive enough money, I would abandon any notion of attending university and make my application to enter nurses' training. It was a time of walking by faith.

I graduated Kincardine District High School in 1955 with the highest marks in my class. As such, I delivered the valedictory speech. It was based on a mountain climbing theme, or maybe it was about climbing a ladder? (Each rung representing a school year.) The bottom line was that our work and effort had led us to a gradual ascent to reach the top, to reach our dream of graduating high school. And having conquered the first mountain, we now had the knowledge and skills to go on to conquer the next.

The papers came for me to apply for a government grant to help with the cost of university. It was a needs-based financial assistance program, and for me to submit the application, I needed the signature of one of my parents.

If I ever wanted to talk with Dad and no one else, I would invite him to join me for a walk. So, I took Dad out for a walk, and along the way, I handed him the papers. As he took them from my hand, I said, "Dad, these papers need your signature. They're for a grant so I can go to university. I want to go to medical school."

He paused. "You know your mother is dead against it?"

"Yes, I know, Dad. I have talked to the Lord. If He wants me to be a doctor, I know I will get enough money for the first year. I'll find enough money for the rest of the years, too." I had placed my situation before him. We finished our walk together. Dad didn't sign the papers that day, he gave himself some time to consider. He was always wise that way, giving himself a moment before he spoke his thoughts. Not knowing his answer, I began to prepare myself for nurses' training. But then, unexpectedly, Dad handed me the papers with his seal of support.

When the government grant was approved, I totalled the sum of my collection. My French teacher had awarded a $100 scholarship to the student with the highest marks in her class—me. As the valedictorian, I was also given another award. The Lord gave me enough for the first year: my tuition fees, textbooks, and a place to stay for the year (room and board were covered).

Mother promised me $200 if I stayed home that summer between high school and university to harvest the strawberries on our house block. It was a small business enterprise, and I picked for about a month. Every day, Dad drove me to Inverhuron to the beach so I could cool off in the high heat of noon. He sat and waited for me. Even though I couldn't exactly swim, I immersed myself in the fresh, cool water of Lake Huron. That summer, I also painted the outside of an old farmhouse, a two-storey home, and earned another $200 for the pot.

Mother's attitude toward university never weakened. She remained obstinately opposed, even until my graduation day. She seemed to forgive me (or at least overlooked my going there) when I later committed myself to work in India. Mother often quoted a verse in the Bible to support her point of view. In the old English of the King James, she would spout, "Honour thy father and thy mother," and triumphantly continue, "and that is the only commandment with a promise!" Perhaps she echoed the teachings of her own mother. As an adult, I agreed with her, but on occasion, I would remind Mother that being obedient to the Lord did not dishonour her—He would always come first.

Medical school was tough, and I was thankful for not having to worry about money as a first year student. I stayed in a boarding house, a difficult adjustment since I didn't know anyone and felt shy. From second year, my days were divided between classes, studying, and working. Little time was left over for any social life to speak of. Although, I did attend a newly formed local church that was meeting in a basement. The people there were genuine. I was also a member of the Inter-Varsity Christian Fellowship group and, when able, I attended the monthly get-together with the Nurses Christian Fellowship.

In the 1950s, women in the school of medicine were an anomaly and were not warmly welcomed by the faculty. As one of four women in our medicine class of sixty, I was not exempt from the professors' contempt. In class, the professors directed questions toward the girls that were intentionally too difficult to answer; we were made to feel uncomfortable by way of humiliation. This only challenged me to work harder to avoid the embarrassment of not knowing. On the other hand, the boys in class respected the girls and treated us as their peers.

We had some memorable moments in anatomy class. There were six students assigned to each cadaver, three on each side. For three hours every afternoon, we dissected and explored the workings of the human body and were tested every week as to our findings. Formaldehyde was used as a preservative. We inhaled and almost tasted the vapours, absorbing the pungent chemical smell into our skin. On one occasion, I misplaced my pen, only to find it carefully positioned in the mouth of our cadaver.

To round off my full timetable of class lectures and laboratory learning, Saturday morning I studied geology from eight-thirty in the morning until noon; it was my elective subject as rocks and earth interested me, far more than calculus!

During the summer when the university was on break, I started working in the laboratories of Victoria Hospital in London, Ontario. While the regular laboratory technicians were on vacation, I covered all their shifts, working the days and the emergency calls through the nights. Among the many tasks I learned, it was a Sunday job to type and crossmatch blood in readiness for the Monday morning abdominal surgeries. Blood for transfusions was stored in glass bottles in the fridge. The hematology and chemistry laboratories were side-by-side on the second floor, with the transfusion laboratory, or blood bank, upstairs on the seventh floor. There was just enough time in the elevator between labs to catch forty winks.

Thrown in at the deep end, my first weekend, I observed the most senior technician draw blood and carry out the laboratory tests. The very next weekend I was put to work, on call, despite not having taken anyone's blood unsupervised. As you can imagine, I was nervous, and my first solo attempt stabbed right through the patient's vein, leaving a large bruise. My second attempt was an improvement, and I quickly mastered a new skill. Tools of the trade were reusable glass syringes and reusable attachable needles that were blunted and dull. I had carefully penned the laboratory procedures in a spiral notebook to carry with me, along with my *Aids to Anatomy* book tucked in the side pocket.

The laboratory work itself involved mixing solutions with blood samples, boiling test tubes over a gas burner with a single open flame, and setting hand-wound alarm clocks. To measure blood sugar, a sample of blood was mixed with a solution and steeped in a hot water bath for seven minutes, enough time for me to fall asleep. That's how exhausted my body was in those days.

One summer, I had been working around the clock. At noon, with the telephone resting beside me, I napped through my allotted forty-five-minute lunch break. My alarm clock sounded, breaking me out of a deep sleep. I picked it up, pressed it against my ear and answered, "Lab technician." It wouldn't have been so memorable except for the fact that my roommates out in the hall had witnessed my mistake and laughed their heads off.

I continued working in the laboratory throughout the academic year, working nights and weekends, resuming full-time work over the summer months. To do this, I moved from the boarding house into a room on the eighth floor of Victoria Hospital.

My final year was more hands on in the field. The schedule was less structured and consumed most of my time. As such, I couldn't continue to work in the laboratory. I had saved enough money and shared an apartment with Anne, a fellow laboratory technician. Sharing living expenses made it manageable.

I graduated in 1961 with my MD (Doctor of Medicine) completely debt-free! Those six years taught me the valuable lesson of trusting the Lord to meet all my needs as I followed Him. A passage from the Bible sums it up well. As recorded in Proverbs, King Solomon wisely writes, "With all your heart you must trust the Lord and not your own judgment. Always let Him lead you, and He will clear the road for you to follow."[4]

Bessie was a registered laboratory technician before she too became a medical doctor. I first met her in the hematology lab, sitting on the island bench in the middle of the room. I was swinging my feet back and forth. Knowing that she was a fellow believer of God, I asked her, "What church do you go to?" After she answered I asked, "What do they believe?"

Her reply amused me then as it does now "Well, they believe the same as the Baptists, but they're not as strict!" University days exposed me to the interfaith community: people from various Christian churches with a shared belief in the same God who also exhibit

---

[4] Proverbs 3:5–6 (CEV)

different approaches to worship practices and moral conduct.

Bessie remembers my helping her to learn Spanish. She needed a foreign language credit for medical school, and I grilled her vocabulary and grammar in between lab tests.

On weekends off, Bessie took me with her to explore places like Algonquin Provincial Park in Ontario. (Living on a shoestring, I didn't have a car then, but Bessie did.) We cooked a can of pork and beans on a BBQ in the park and slept in the car—one in the front seat, and one in the back. We parked in gas stations and used their facilities. That was in the days before gas stations locked their toilets and attached the key to a wheel cap or a rusty old wrench.

We wandered over marked trails and soaked in the beautiful scenery. Deer and black bears crossed the path. Some deer approached us and took food from our hand, but we kept a wide berth of the bears and respected their territory. We enjoyed our little jaunts around Ontario.

I remember Bessie attending my graduation day. She and Anne stood in as surrogate parents that day to celebrate my finishing medical school. I could invite two people to witness my graduation ceremony. First, I asked Mother and Dad, but Mother remained convinced that university was the place of the devil; her inability to attend kept Dad from coming too. Mother was unable to set foot on the university grounds where our ceremony was held, to do so would have been in contradiction to her religion.

With eight siblings in total, it wasn't possible to choose only two. So, I asked two of my best friends to join me, Bessie and Anne. Aside from the pomp of wearing a cap and gown and receiving my diploma, we medical graduates also attended a smaller ceremony where we recited the Hippocratic Oath. Following the graduation formalities, including a tree-planting ceremony, my family hosted a celebration in my brother Gordon and sister-in-law Anne's home in London, Ontario. Mother and Dad joined the get-together there. Although Mother conceded to attend on the grounds that the celebration was held in my brother's home, she did not willingly participate. She spent the day resting in bed with ailment. Setting aside her antics, we feasted, and I delighted in my family's embrace of my achievement.

From my first disastrous day at elementary school, the Lord accomplished far more than I ever imagined or dreamed about as a child. Having positioned myself to become a teacher, I miraculously graduated medical school. To this day I am amazed that I succeeded! My brothers and sisters were an inspiration to me, as I endeavoured to live out the opportunities they had longed for through the opportunity I had been given. Growing up, it was a huge hurdle for me to even arrive at secondary school. University had never been a mealtime conversation, and subsistence farm life could not pay for an education. Besides, studying medicine was traditionally for the boys.

The privilege of my education was the foundation of my adult years and life's work. This foundation stands as the third memorial stone of God's grace toward me. It demonstrates His provision and His equipping me for the journey. God determines our days and the life path ahead. If we acknowledge Him and trust Him, He will show us the way we should go. With allegiance to the Hippocratic Oath and a promise to God to do whatever He asked, I launched into medical work.

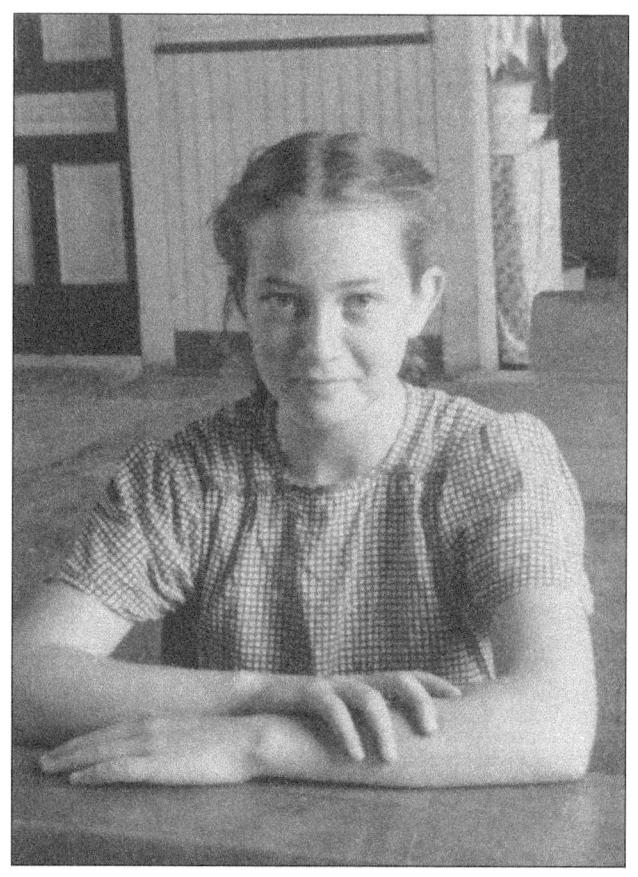

Elementary School

*Graduation 1961
Anne, Aletta & Bessie*

High School Graduation
Front Page

KINETTE PRIZE WINNERS

Grade IX — Alberta Wightman	$10
Grade X — Bernice Collins	$10
Grade XI — Deanna Doupe	$10
Grade XII — Cliff Hewitt	$10
Grade XIII — Aletta Bell	$100

SCHOLARSHIPS

Aletta Bell:	Dominion Provincial University Bursary	$500
	Atkinson Foundation Bursary	$400
	University of Western Ontario Scholarship	$200
Diane MacDonald:	Dominion Provincial Grade XIII Bursary	$100

TROPHY WINNERS

Girls' Field Day Champions   (Mr. and Mrs. Gordon Cottrill)
    Junior: Mary Thornicroft   Intermediate: Shirley Bennett
            Senior: Helen Farley

Boys' Field Day Champions   (Mickey Baker and Bill Irwin)
    Junior: Beven McLean   Intermediate: Ronald Parkinson
            Senior: William Gottschalk

Valedictorian   (Roy Ross and Les Petter)   -   -   Aletta Bell

High School Graduation
Back Page

1955 Painting Tiverton home

Remember your leaders who taught you the word of God. Think of all the good that has come from their lives, and follow the example of their faith.

Hebrews 13:7 (NLT)

FELLOWSHIP

As I pulled the covers over me, the complications that cluttered my mind quieted, and in the darkened room, the noise of the day faded into sleep. After coming off a twenty-four-hour shift in the obstetric department, I was comatose. Not more than an hour had passed since my head sank into the pillow when the telephone, wired in beside me, buzzed. I picked up the receiver and croaked out, "Dr. Bell speaking."

The switchboard operator announced, "There is a Dr. Hemwall here to see you. He says he is visiting from Chicago." I groped for my glasses, as if being able to see while talking on the telephone would help me to remember who he was. As the fog of slumber began to clear, I remembered his name. I had seen it written somewhere.

"Okay, tell him I'll meet him in the lobby." My head was heavy with fatigue. I donned clothes, pulled a comb through my hair, and made my way downstairs.

―⁂―

Having graduated medical school, the next step was to consolidate my knowledge so that I could live out my healing vocation. I began with a one-year internship at Victoria Hospital, where I had previously worked as a laboratory technician and studied as a medical student. The marathon of sleepless nights continued, followed by full days of work and the grind of being young, new, and female.

As the earth made its annual orbit around the sun, I began to look ahead for the next foothold; I continued to want to walk in the Lord's footprints. At the end of the year, after having completed my internship, I would qualify to set up a private practice. I could hang up my shingle, so to speak: "Aletta G. Bell, MD." However, I had sensed that I would work in a foreign country where medical service was lacking. To do this, I realized that I needed more experience, so I took the necessary steps to prepare myself. I decided that a general practice (GP) residency would improve my clinical knowledge and hone my practical skills. At that time, Canada offered only two or three placements in GP residencies, so I expanded my search to the United States.

Open to the adventure of travel, I wrote a letter of inquiry to the director of the Christian Medical Society[1] in the United States. (Previously, a representative of the society had come to Canada and talked to a group of medical students at a meeting in Toronto. Interested, I had signed up as a member.) In my letter, I asked if there were any GP residency programs that would help prepare me for work outside of North America. The

---

[1] Now known as the Christian Medical & Dental Associations.

director replied with the names and contact details of doctors who were members of the Christian Medical Society and who could assist me in my search.

One of the names was Dr. Gus Hemwall. He was affiliated with West Suburban Hospital in Oak Park, Illinois, a western neighbourhood of Chicago. West Suburban had a GP residency program, but Dr. Hemwall did not wait for me to contact him.

Aware of my letter of inquiry to the society in December of 1961, he just happened to be passing through London, Ontario, and stopped in to introduce himself. Sleep deprived and unprepared, I met him in the lobby. I liked him from that first meeting. He was a kindly gentleman with a quiet persistent way about him.

He told me that West Suburban had a good GP residency program, and he encouraged me to come and see for myself. With Christmas holidays approaching, I agreed to visit. As an intern, I had the choice of five days leave to take either at Christmas time or around New Year's. Since my family always came together at Christmas, I chose this time for my five-day break. I decided to squeeze in a quick trip to Chicago before Christmas Day.

Earning money as an intern, I was able to purchase a second-hand Vauxhall car for $900. After one or two driving lessons, I passed my driver's licence test by turning right, turning left, not driving too fast, and pulling into a parking space. However, I essentially learned to drive by putting 5,000 miles[2] on the odometer. In the first 1,000 miles[3] I drove to Chicago on a reconnaissance tour with one of my best friends from university, Bessie.

Days before Christmas, we hatched the plan to drive from London to Chicago where we would stay overnight, investigate West Suburban's GP residency program, and drive back home in time for our respective family's Christmas celebrations. We shared the driving, arriving safely in the evening, and camped in a cheap motel in the vicinity of West Suburban. There had been no hint of snow on our journey there, but when we woke the next morning, an abundance of snow blanketed the city—we could not even see the car! Unfortunately, I was not yet acquainted with driving in the winter. I didn't even own a snow brush or a shovel, and a snowplow had pushed past the Vauxhall, banking the snow over our car.

We spent the day at West Suburban Hospital. Dr. Hemwall introduced me to the head of the GP residency program, and we discussed the formalities of my taking a position there. I was impressed by the facilities and looked forward to starting.

It was late when we set out on our return journey. The road was hazardous, coming home across the Interstate 94. So much so that when I pressed on the brakes, I slid into a car in front of me. Thankfully, there

---

[2] 8,047 kilometres
[3] 1,609 kilometres

was no damage to either vehicle as our snail's pace had cushioned the impact.

Bessie was asleep when a red-light indicator suddenly came on. I knew nothing about cars then, and so I poked Bessie awake, "What's that red light?" She was quick to identify that the generator light was on, so we pulled off the Interstate at Albion, Michigan. It was late in the night. A guy at the gas station checked the car over. The generator was worn out. He did not have a replacement because the Vauxhall was a British car. He gave us two options: go back to Chicago or on to Detroit for a new generator. We took a third option and stayed overnight in a motel, leaving the Vauxhall to be picked up later. The next day, we bused back to London and picked up Bessie's car.

Bessie drove me home to Kincardine and then made her way home to Beamsville, adding at least three hours to her usual route. Two things I learned from that trip: if I decided to live and work in the United States, I would need a more serviceable car and it is not wise to make such a long journey to be home for Christmas—it had exhausted me!

I began my GP residency at West Suburban Hospital in July 1962. It was a two-year program. My learning extended well beyond my doctoring skills as I formed new relationships with others who believed in God. Raised a Baptist, I inherently looked for a Baptist church in the Oak Park area. However, in the big metropolis of Chicago, I discovered more than one kind of Baptist church, and finding a place to meet with people on Sunday proved to be perplexing.

For the first three months, every Sunday morning that I was free from work, I visited a different Baptist church until I began to wonder what kind of Baptist I was. In my area alone, there were the Southern Baptists, the Northern Baptists, the Swedish Baptists, the Strict Baptists, the Regular Baptists, and the Water Baptists. One held to an undocumented dress code, like all the ladies had to wear a hat. Another adhered to the King James translation of the Bible as the *only* Bible without error. There was something uniquely specific about each one. Exasperated and confused with my search, I voiced my complaint to a nurse who lived in the same hospital accommodation as me. She encouraged me to come to her church. "What kind of church do you go to?" I asked her with a weary and skeptical tone.

"I go to a Bible church," she answered plainly.

"A Bible church?" I repeated with a little more animation. "I thought they were all supposed to teach the Bible?!" (At that point, I had much to learn.) Suffice to say, I accompanied my nurse friend to her "Bible church," and my search happily ended there at Calvary Memorial Church (CMC).

From the first day, I enjoyed the fellowship of the people at CMC. The other churches I had visited had not greeted me—no one had even offered a handshake. But CMC offered a warm, sustaining welcome that kept me there, and I enjoyed the Bible teaching. It was the beginning of a lifelong fellowship with CMC, a church with an interdenominational foundation. The God of my childhood was the same God of my young adulthood; my understanding of Him and my relationship with Him deepened as I spent time with Him and His people.

CMC gathered to encourage one another, but they also reached out to people in their community and even beyond to people who lived overseas. In their effort to meet the physical and spiritual needs of people, they shared the love of God with them. Their compassion toward others reminded me of my childhood promise to God: to do whatever He asked me to do if He saved my dog, Trixie.

When Trixie recovered, the eyes of my heart opened to God. In that moment, unlike Mother's list of unbreakable rules, God revealed His grace toward me. Despite my waywardness and my inability to follow all the rules, He healed my most treasured childhood friend. With my heart committed to keeping my promise and open to His leading, God guided me from a hand-to-mouth existence on the farm to graduation from medical school.

It seemed a natural progression to use what I had to help others, specifically those disadvantaged by abject poverty and deprived of basic medical care. Through an expanding web of connections in Chicago, I began to explore ways to work in a foreign country. However, during my GP residency, alongside my desire to work in a foreign country, I was earning $400 a month and owned a car. Material things began to grip me, and I enjoyed the luxury of a disposable income. Although my ambition remained, it began to fade. My aspirations to work elsewhere slowly dissolved into my comfortable life in Chicago.

During that time, Dr. Hemwall employed me. In the evenings, after I had finished work, if I was not on call at West Suburban, I would join him in his private practice. On the weekends, he allowed me to look after his patients in the hospital, and when he referred patients to a specialist, I was the go-between.

Dr. Hemwall was a great man, and I learned the art of medicine from him. He encouraged and guided me. In his lifetime, Dr. Hemwall travelled to five continents—not for pleasure, but to provide humanitarian aid. The governments of Liberia, Korea, and Honduras presented him with awards for his charitable work in their countries. He demonstrated the care of the whole person.

Doing rounds with Dr. Hemwall and visiting his patients in the hospital provided an invaluable lesson in the practice of medicine. Hospital rounds are a review of the patient's status and treatment, and Dr. Hemwall's approach to patients was different from any other doctor I had observed or trained under. Rather than standing at the foot of the bed, he would sit down on a chair at the head of the bed.

In those days, boxes of chocolates gifted to patients by their family and friends were commonplace. On doctor's rounds with Dr. Hemwall, he would pick up a box of chocolates from a patient's bedside cabinet and offer me one. With the patient's box of chocolates in his hands, he would ask them how they were feeling. By sitting down beside them at their same level, Dr. Hemwall put his patients at ease. He showed them that he was not in a hurry, and so they relaxed. From this position, his patients were able to express themselves, and there was a meaningful exchange of information. He adjusted treatment plans in collaboration with the patient; these plans were known to be much more effective.

Dr. Hemwall was a general practitioner, not a surgeon. Even so, he had permission to perform surgery at West Suburban Hospital. Interestingly, his patients were known to recover well and mostly without complications. Under his tutelage, he gave me the opportunity to do surgery, and I learned how to tie surgical knots with a shorter length of suture material. (Dr. Hemwall knew that medical supplies in a foreign country were in short supply, so he taught me how to conserve my resources.)

Dr. Hemwall also imparted his profound respect for tissue while doing surgery. His gentle handling of tissue caused less injury and shortened healing time. He would retract the skin or hold an organ out of the way with the softness of fingers, rather than the hardness of metal retractors. I learned and practised this technique with him. Patients who had their gallbladders removed by Dr. Hemwall recovered much more quickly than the patients of surgeons.

At that time, it was normal practice to insert a nasogastric tube[4] in every patient after gallbladder removal surgery. But Dr. Hemwall never followed this practice. His standing order was "NPO and fluids as tolerated."[5] When I asked him why, he simply said, "We do not touch the gut that much in removing the gallbladder. Any patient with a nasogastric tube is not happy."

Dr. Hemwall exemplified his faith in God. Among the many things he taught me about the practice of medicine, including the holistic care of the patient, Dr. Hemwall showed me how to live out the second commandment of Jesus, "Love your neighbour as yourself." (The first command is to love God with all your heart, all your soul, and all your mind.) [6]

I clearly remember Dr. Hemwall's generous response to an American man (a fellow doctor who had been working in China) who had returned home to Chicago because he was unwell with tuberculosis. To my recollection, he had also suffered a heart attack. This fellow doctor was a father of two young sons. In poor health and unable to work or to borrow money, the doctor was powerless to provide for his family: he was in dire need. Dr. Hemwall heard about this man's

---

[4] A thin tube passed from the nose to the stomach to drain the accumulation of irritating gastric fluids, or in reverse, it can be used as a feeding tube.
[5] NPO means "nothing by mouth." It comes from the abbreviation of the Latin words, *nil per os.*
[6] Matthew 22:36–40 (NLT)

predicament and visited him. He offered him a job in his private practice. Dr. Hemwall started paying him his salary while he was still recovering in the tuberculosis sanatorium. As a result, the man was able to care for and educate his sons. One son became a laboratory technician and the other became a medical doctor. Both sons dedicated their lives to work in poorer countries. I learned a great deal from Dr. Hemwall.

At West Suburban Hospital I also met Dr. Marvin Tiesenga. He was a surgeon who offered his professional services at the Cook County Jail in Chicago, Illinois. (The prison was once residence to Al Capone, a famous gangster first incarcerated there in 1931.) Dr. Tiesenga wanted to help prepare me for charity work abroad, and so he took me with him to the jail to practise my surgical skills.

The facilities were atrocious; I had never seen anything like it. They reflected the slum areas of Chicago at that time. It was a good introduction to what awaited me in India. Although India's living standards would be far more atrocious, it somehow jolted me into a greater understanding of people's vulnerability and suffering. Inmates near death were moved into a separate room, dying alone. That shocked me, and even now the memory of those men tossed aside reverberates.

There was a small team who staffed the prison hospital, but my experience there was strictly surgical. I only worked in the operating room; I was there for the procedure, not for any follow-up care, and there was no preoperative consult. We used ether, a simple, cost-effective compound for general anesthesia. (At the time, it was relatively safe to use as the dose required to induce anesthesia was much less than the dose that could become potentially toxic.)

On one occasion, Dr. Tiesenga took me with him to the county jail to fix a broken hip. We had no X-ray machine or access to one. Hip surgery was a messy business with blood oozing everywhere. With my gloved hands and surgical gown soaked in blood, I had located the broken area and was preparing to hammer in the pins when Dr. Tiesenga spoke up from across the operating table, "Just remember, you have to clean up this mess." It was a surreal experience, but in a way, it grounded me for performing surgery without standard conveniences like X-ray machines or the full support of a surgical team.

In my early years of medicine, God's people encouraged me in faith, keeping faith central to my pursuits. It has been said that "no man is an island," and in my experience this principle rings true—fellowship is key.[7] As the Apostle Paul espoused, "Don't stop meeting together with other believers. . . Instead, encourage each other. . ."[8] Fellowship is vital to a personal, dynamic, and living faith. It stretches beyond shared common beliefs and attitudes; it is a deep

---

[7] Donne, John, "No Man Is an Island," *Devotions Upon Emergent Occasions—Meditation XVII*, 1624.

[8] Hebrews 10:25 (CEB)

connectedness with other believers of God by way of His Spirit. Without fellowship, we cannot be encouraged, supported, or cheered on! Dr. Hemwall, Dr. Tiesenga, and the people at CMC shared Christian fellowship with me. Without their encouragement and guidance—without their fellowship—the allure of a comfortable life may not have loosened its grip. Fellowship is essential to the preservation of our faith and our endeavours.

Years later when I was working in India, God would continue to provide the sustenance of fellowship for me. Without which, I would likely have given up many times. Living in rural, impoverished India, the enormity of suffering surrounded me. Adapting to cultural differences, extreme heat, and language barriers constantly challenged me. The fellowship of believers enabled me to continue in my vocation, and the prayers of God's people sustained me. Difficulties in life happen, and although we can individually cling to our faith in God and know that He will sustain us, how much better it is to stand together. The wisdom of King Solomon sums this up well: "Two people are better off than one, for they can help each other succeed."[9]

Living abroad, physically separated from my family of believers, did not dampen the fellowship we shared. However, communication between countries was

---

[9] Ecclesiastes 4:9–12 (NLT): "Two people are better off than one, for they can help each other succeed. If one person falls, the other can reach out and help. But someone who falls alone is in real trouble. Likewise, two people lying close together can keep each other warm. But how can one be warm alone? A person standing alone can be attacked and defeated, but two can stand back-to-back and conquer. Three are even better, for a triple-braided cord is not easily broken."

challenging. Nowadays, virtual connection is commonplace, and it is almost incomprehensible that it was once exceedingly difficult—and sometimes impossible—to telephone someone who lived far away. A letter sent by snail mail took weeks to arrive. Or, as often happened, the postal service lost, stole, or destroyed letters. Virtual communities and social media platforms did not exist. Text messaging and a telephone with video camera display were science fiction. And so, any successful telephone connection—no matter how crackly or broken up the conversation—any letter or parcel that arrived in my hands, or any face-to-face visit encouraged me, filling me with joy and emboldening me to continue.

People expected me to stay in touch with them, yet they did not always stay in touch with me. But those who did write to me warmed my soul. One lady from CMC, Ruth, wrote me a letter every week. Her letters were a link to home and to the community of believers who knew me. Although she wrote as a representative of CMC, her letters always included a personal exchange and a reassurance or an inspiration from the Scriptures. Reading her letters cheered me on and raised my spirits in difficult days.

I welcomed visitors to India with a standing invitation: if anyone felt adventuresome, I invited them to come and see. One of my most memorable visits was that of Pastor Ray and his wife, Marlene. (Pastor Ray was the pastor of Calvary Memorial Church.) Two nurses from the congregation joined them in their travels. Their visit was a tangible encouragement and help to me. Although their expedition to India personally challenged them, their physical presence was of great personal significance. My life in India was a constant outpouring of effort and giving into the lives of those around me. When Ray and Marlene (and others) visited me, I had the joy and excitement of showing them where I worked and introducing them to the people I had embraced. Their being there was like soft rain falling on dry ground.

Ray and Marlene's journey was not without effort, cost, and suffering. To this day, they assert that they were not prepared for India. They endured the discomfort of travel, including flat tires and the nonexistence of bathrooms. They crossed an international road border from Nepal into India with their mouths wide open—their passport details handwritten into a big green ledger. Everything about India overwhelmed them: their five physical senses were saturated by the throng of people and poverty, and they sensed the thick oppression of spiritual darkness that pulsed in the air. They had entered the poorest state of India, and what they saw imprinted in their thoughts and hearts. Navigating language barriers and using interpreters, Ray was able to teach and encourage fellow believers while Marlene met with a special gathering of women.

When I met up with Ray and Marlene some twenty-one years later in their home in Dallas, Texas, Ray so poignantly described to me, "Once you move past the culture shock, the language shock, the religion shock, the food shock—*all* the other shocks! Once you finally begin to process all of that, then you travel out into the villages, and you realize that is where light meets darkness. The Light has come into the world and the darkness cannot overcome it."

Fellowship was strengthened and sustained by way of visits home to North America and through presentations about my work in India. Meeting together and sharing my experiences with CMC and other local churches, reinforced our bond; we encouraged each other. The first time I travelled back to CMC from India in 1968, I stood at the front of the church, facing the people. (At that time, CMC gathered in a building on Madison Street.) Taken aback, I was struck by the lines of perfectly white pews adorned with plush red cushions. I suddenly felt like I did not belong. As I spoke, Hindi words broke up my English sentences, and the audience responded with blank stares. I stammered through my presentation. It felt peculiar to struggle to communicate in my mother tongue. Looking back, I realize it was my first experience of reverse culture shock. My life had been rooted in India for almost four years, long enough for language and culture to transform my perception of the world around me. India had changed me forever, and forevermore, neither India nor Canada nor America was my true home. "For this world is not our permanent home; we are looking forward to a home yet to come."[10]

---

[10] Hebrews 13:14 (NLT)

As a foreigner (a Canadian in the United States), I was accepted by CMC as part of their family. That has always been very meaningful for me, much more than I am able to express. CMC has supported me from the first step that I took toward India, right up until today. I am incredibly grateful for their devotion to prayer, their fellowship, and their very practical financial care.

In Canada, a small church in Cannington, Ontario, also faithfully provided fellowship and continues to care for me, even now. A fellow graduate of medical school, Ivan, had set up his medical practice in Cannington. He and his wife had attended Bible School, and in our student days, Ivan talked with me about his aspirations to work in a foreign country to help the poor. One time when I was home in North America, on leave from my work in India, I phoned Ivan.

"When are you going to take your doctoring overseas?" I challenged him with a chuckle.

"I haven't got anyone to cover my practice," he said.

"I'm available!"

And so it happened, I covered Ivan's practice for several months while he volunteered in Africa. During my stay in Cannington, I attended Cannington Baptist Church. From that brief interlude, they embraced the passion for my work in India, keeping contact with me, praying for me, and financially supporting me.

Through the years, fellowship with God's people was fortified when they accommodated me in their homes.

That was the old way. When I visited the churches who supported my work, people warmly welcomed me into their homes. Staying with them gave us opportunity to talk and to form lifelong relationships. Nowadays, people host guests in a nearby hotel, and it is more common for them to take you out for meals. The closeness of fellowship and the dynamic of relationship has altered as there is much less opportunity to interact personally with one another.

Staying with host families not only encouraged me but also significantly impacted my hosts. Somewhere between the late 1970s and the early 1980s, I attended Calvary Memorial Church's annual conference for the workers they supported overseas. A young family opened their home for the first time. They were interested to learn more about the workers they prayed for each week and supported financially, and I was the first to accept their invitation.

Around that time, a new book was popular among Christians in North America. It challenged wealthy Christians on their point of view and participation in worldwide poverty and hunger. With the subject of poverty and hunger at the forefront, people were interested in my attitude and approach.

The young family I stayed with comprised of two fun and energetic boys. Their home was palatial, and many rooms were more decorative than functional. And although their hospitality was warm and very generous, I wondered how they viewed their rich lifestyle when I talked with them about the poverty I knew in India.

During my stay with them, Moody Radio, a Christian radio network that broadcasts from Chicago, interviewed me about my work in India. The interviewer asked me what wealthy Christians could do to help feed the poor. Of course, my first point was "Well, you don't have to live in a big house!" My plain-spoken answer influenced my hosts as they downsized from their home and never again lived in a big house.

The external changes they made inspired their ensuing life choices as they followed the path the Lord had ahead of them. The immediate impact that was the most astounding and remarkable to me was when my host took me to Jewellers Row on Wabash Avenue. Nestled in the historic buildings was (and still is) an area of upscale jewellery stores, specializing in diamonds. She sold her personal collection of diamond-adorned jewellery and handed me the earnings—thousands of dollars to buy essential medical equipment for my workplace in India!

Aside from my being totally blown away, my hosts lives were changed forever. For them, it was the beginning of inner-city work, reaching deep into the lives of the poor and needy in their community. Having left their palatial fortress, their lives opened to the lives of others less fortunate than themselves. This encounter (and others like it) demonstrates how God's love is displayed through the unity of fellowship.

Another noteworthy visitor to me in India was Dr. Hemwall and his wife. His continued fellowship and nurture of me was significant. Nine years had passed since we last worked together in Chicago, and *nineteen* years had passed since my residency there. In 1982, after attending an international congress of Christian physicians in Bangalore,[11] South India, Dr. Hemwall and his wife made the journey up to North India where I worked. It was a joy to see them and to host them for one whole week.

They carried with them news and views from home, and Dr. Hemwall rolled up his sleeves and worked. He used his prolotherapy technique to cure headaches, back aches, and joint pains (including my painful shoulder that I had injured picking up a baby goat).

Our time together flashed by, and I tried to learn his prolotherapy techniques. In a way, I had already adapted Dr. Hemwall's teachings to my doctoring in India. He had once shown me the power of touch in the process of healing. In India, it was not culturally appropriate for me to go around patting a man on the back, but it was okay for "the doctor" to take a pulse. So, it was possible to have contact and to use touch to communicate empathy, establish trust, and show that I cared. And feeling a pulse, tells you a great deal more than reading a number off a monitor.

Nearing the end of his earthly life, I met up with Dr. Hemwall at a conference held at Calvary Memorial Church. He was an old man, shuffling along unaided (although his wife told me that he was supposed to be using a cane). I was home in North America on leave

---

[11] Officially known as Bengaluru.

and was speaking about my work in India in the big auditorium. Dr. Hemwall was there to listen, and I was able to honour him for what he had done for me, for the things he had taught me, and for the encouragement he had given me.

Significantly, Dr. Hemwall recognized that God was leading me to work outside of North America. Without knowing, he encouraged me to keep my childhood promise to God. Dr. Hemwall taught me by the example of his life, his work, and his faith. Without his influence, his care, his genuine interest, and the fellowship that we shared in our love for God and each other, I would not have found the path I walked.

My relationship with God's people sustained me. I could not have endured in my work without their closeness and constant support. Their prayers kept me going during hot and difficult days in India. When my workload became very heavy, physical exhaustion often kept me from regular correspondence. During those hassled times, I was in more urgent need of prayers than at any other time. I depended on the fellowship of God's people; my work was not possible without them.

At Christmas time especially, I appreciated letters and cards that reminded me people were praying for me and supporting me wholeheartedly in my effort. Their messages were a genuine encouragement to me. Even now in my old age, birthday greetings continue to sustain me. It is wonderful to belong to the family of God.

My years in India were not a solo flight; I have achieved nothing on my own. God has been with me and piloted my course, and His people have stood with me and encouraged me. They have prayed and continue to pray for me; they have shared and continue to share their material resources with me. And they have walked with me as family. God's people prepared, guided, and supported me in my quest to work in a foreign country. The fellowship of God's people, the spiritual union by way of the Holy Spirit, stands as the fourth memorial stone of God's grace in my life.

1964 Reception at Oak Park Country Club, Chicago
L to R: Dr. Nichols, Dr. Bell, Dr. Tiesenga & Dr. Hemwall

Friends Honour Doctor Leaving For India

A note in the Chicago Tribune recently, told of the plans of a Tiverton native, Dr. Aletta Bell, daughter of Mr. and Mrs. Daniel Bell, of Tiverton.

A group of doctors from the West Suburban Hospital there are giving a recpetion honouring staff member Dr. Aletta Bell, at Oak Park Country Club in Chicago on Sunday, October 25. Dr. G. A. Hemwell and Dr. E. E. Nichols are in charge.

Dr. Bell, a resident physician, returned a year ago from a tenure in the Middle East as a missionary doctor and now has signed up for a five year term in India sponsored by the Ceylon and India Mission.

Her friends presented Miss Bell with a purse containing $300 and her fare to New York.

1964 Newspaper Clipping

I've commanded you to be strong and brave. Don't ever be afraid or discouraged! I am the Lord your God, and I will be there to help you wherever you go.

Joshua 1:9 (CEV)

FOCUS

Last century, air travel was considered a life event—ladies dressed up for the occasion. Trussed in a new pair of silk stockings, a two-piece outfit, and flat-heeled shoes, I paused on the landing of the aircraft steps and positioned myself for a photograph. A blurred image captures me looking back, with an elegant wave of my right hand.

Onboard, I smoothed my skirt and slid into the window seat. Sitting there, waiting to be thrust into the sky, I began to wonder, what in the world I was doing. I said to myself, *Aletta, you must be crazy!* Thoughts tumbled in my mind as the airplane lifted its wheels from the runway. I peered out the window and watched the landscape grow smaller until it disappeared behind a layer of clouds.

The airplane reached altitude and levelled itself for the journey. With the last-minute flurry of packing and goodbyes behind me, I now sat captive somewhere above the Atlantic Ocean. I shook my head in contemplation and released a long deep breath. I pondered the three things I knew about Arabia: it was hot, it was mostly desert, and camels lived there.

At age twenty-six, nearing the middle of my residency at West Suburban Hospital, I arrived for work one evening in Dr. Hemwall's private practice. He popped his head in and said, "I need to see you before you go home tonight." My heart sank immediately as I thought I must have done something terribly wrong.

Under his supervision and encouragement, my confidence in the practice of medicine had strengthened. After a short time, Dr. Hemwall began to trust me with the care of his patients during his periods of leave. Not fully licensed, I wasn't able to write prescriptions for narcotics. So, he left me with a bunch of signed prescription pads to use while he was away. Perhaps I had prescribed the wrong drug; my mind was troubled, and I worried about his summons the whole time I was seeing patients.

My imaginings reached their peak by the close of business, and I met Dr. Hemwall in his office as requested. We sat down together with coffee in hand. He had a very wooden, straight-faced expression when he announced, "One of us has to go to Arabia!" Dr. Hemwall, a quiet Swedish man, was known to appreciate a joke and could serve up humour without warning.

The combination of his serious tone and the thought of one of us going to Arabia triggered a chuckle, and I quipped back, "Oh yes, I've always wanted to go to Arabia!" When he didn't join in my laughter, I realized his proposal was real. My chuckle hung awkwardly in the air. I leaned back and said, "Well *I* can't go."

His face softened, and he continued with an explanation. He told me that a sheik had given permission for a foreign Christian charity to establish a hospital in the Buraimi Oasis in the Trucial States, now the United Arab Emirates. The sheik had also approved for the charity to tell the people about Jesus, stating that nobody would believe the stories about Him anyway. A doctor and his wife who had started a small hospital were home in the United States on leave, and the locum who was covering had been medically evacuated. The hospital was temporarily without a doctor. Another locum was urgently needed to cover for at least two months, leaving as soon as possible within the next few weeks.

Realizing his seriousness, I began to make excuses as to why I couldn't go. "There is no way that I can go!" I repeated. He politely listened to my reasons. Aside from the fact that my knowledge of Arabia was absolutely zilch (except that it was hot and sandy), there were three obvious arguments against my going. First, I did not have a passport. (In those days, a passport wasn't needed for a Canadian to cross the border into the United States. I had a student visa that allowed me to work and study there during my residency.) Second, I was in the middle of my residency program. Inexperienced, I didn't have the confidence to innovate, to do things I hadn't done before. I would be the only doctor in the middle of the desert. And third, I wasn't immunized. I imagined I would need a great many immunizations to travel there, and as my parents had not consented to childhood shots, I would be starting from the very beginning. Dr. Hemwall seemed to accept my resolution of the matter.

Having started my day early at the hospital and then worked with Dr. Hemwall that evening, I was relieved when my cheek finally pressed against the pillow. But to my surprise, sleep did not come. There have never been many nights when I cannot sleep. Waking up has always been my struggle, not sleeping. With the noise and routine of the day, God sometimes used the quiet and inactive hours of the night to communicate with me. It is easier to listen without distraction. Despite the heaviness of my eyelids, my mind wrestled with the idea of Arabia. There was a bud of excitement, but the barriers to my going seemed immovable. Much later, I learned that others working in Arabia had gathered to pray for a doctor in the hours I had lain awake.

Several days to a week later, I bumped into Dr. Hemwall in the medicine room. Nothing more had been said by either of us concerning Arabia. "By the way, who did you get to go to Arabia?" I quizzed.

Without hesitation he said, "Nobody. When are you leaving?" I was annoyed that my casual remark was reflected back to me as a challenge. To excuse myself, I reminded Dr. Hemwall that I couldn't just pick up and leave in the middle of my residency program. He quietly said, "How do you know? Did you ask?"

Doubtful I replied, "Ok, I'll ask them—but I still don't have a passport, and I expect that would take months."

Again, he responded calmly, "How do you know? Did you ask?"

How else could I answer except to say, "Well ok, I'll ask—and what about my immunizations? There isn't enough time."

Unperturbed he said, "Well, I can line those up for you pretty fast."

Early the next morning, I telephoned the Canadian consulate and asked them how quickly I could arrange a passport. They informed me about three months. To be sure, I continued, explaining my situation and the urgent need for a doctor to travel to Arabia. They told me that in some instances, they could prioritize and produce a passport within three weeks of applying. So, it was possible.

In pursuit of answers, I met with the chief doctor of the residency program. Again, I explained my situation and asked if I would be able to take two-months' leave of absence. He paused for a moment and then looked me straight in the eye. "Do you want to go?" he questioned. In that moment, I realized that I didn't really know. It was strange—I had been so busy erecting obstacles as to why I couldn't go that I hadn't really decided if I wanted to.

Somewhat taken aback, I answered, "Well, I don't really know." His response left the decision solely in my lap.

"If you don't want to go, you can use me as an excuse. On the other hand, if you want to go, you can have the leave and just make up the time at the end." The Lord didn't want me in Arabia by default or by some unseen hand of fate; He needed me to decide whether He was asking me to go. And was I willing? The opportunity was mine to choose, and initially, I declined the invitation, but in the end, God showed me that what I had dismissed as impossible was to become one of the most significant experiences in my life.

I returned to Dr. Hemwall and gave him my answer. "I guess I am going," I told him. Everything moved whiz-bang! Dr. Hemwall didn't hesitate to line me up as a pin cushion, and my immune system kicked into high gear. The needles to protect me against typhoid and smallpox made me particularly unwell. The typhoid shot triggered a high fever within a few hours. Several days later, after I had my smallpox shot, I decided to drive home to my parents in Kincardine (about an eight-hour drive each way) to tell them in person the news of my intended travels. Mother approved and Dad gave his blessing.

On the drive back to Chicago, fever and a muscle ache that seeped into my bones plagued my whole body, and I drove like a maniac. I didn't care whether I lived or died. The police never pulled me over despite my high speed. Next morning, I staggered into work and was promptly given permission to go home to bed. It was a rough several weeks preparation, and within a month, I was alive and well and on my way!

There was no time for any orientation or guidance to help me adjust to my new position. At the airport, Dr. Hemwall advised me to take out travel insurance. "What's that for?" I questioned, having not set foot outside North America.

"Just in case the airplane falls out of the sky, or something happens," he explained. A little puzzled as to the benefit of insurance to me if the airplane fell out of the sky, I complied. It was the first time I had ever been on an airplane in my life! And having boarded the airplane, my mind whirled in a flurry of doubts. I cradled my sanity as I wondered why I had agreed to fly halfway around the world to work in a desert. I knew nobody there, and I had no idea what sort of medical problems I would encounter. I hadn't even considered language barriers and cultural differences.

Flying with British Overseas Airway Corporation (BOAC) was first class treatment. I enjoyed the service and the food. We landed in Bahrain, and I had five hours to explore before boarding my connecting flight to Abu Dhabi, so I decided to take myself on a walking tour. Completely naive to world travel, I had absolutely no idea how hot it would be! When I stepped outside, the steam began to rise, and I slid over the pavement like butter melting in a hot pan. I walked maybe one block and retreated to the air-conditioned cool of the hotel. I couldn't take the heat.

A small twin-engine airplane took me on to Abu Dhabi. The vibration of the engines quickened my heartbeat as the loud pulsing hum whirred in my ears.

We flew low, and my eyes feasted on the expanse. I saw the shadows of clouds on the earth and ships floating in the ocean. The airplane landed in the desert sand—there was no runway—and the 1963 terminal was nothing more than a small brick building with a flat concrete roof. The whitewash was peeling, and burlap walls were draped in one corner. A far cry from the international hub my niece Lydia would later encounter in 2019 when her flight touched down on a modern asphalt and concrete runway, leading to an air-conditioned terminal.

The dry desert heat wilted me, and I thought my stockings had baked onto my legs. A Canadian couple collected me and drove me in a jeep to the Buraimi Oasis where the hospital was located. As we drove into the desert, there were no roads that I could see, only tire tracks in the sand. There was no air-conditioning in the jeep. We came to a wooden signpost with two arrows: one pointed to the left, and one pointed to the right. The husband-and-wife team sent to fetch me pulled up and debated which way we should turn. Sweltering in the heat of being stationary, I prayed, *Lord, save me from this desert place. My guides don't even know which way they should go!*

On our journey to the hospital, I saw date palms, and scrub bushes, and the skeleton of a camel bleached white by the sun. There was a far distant mountain range, a bruised ripple on the horizon. We came across a fellow traveller with a goat in his back seat, standing on a load of cut bushes with some resemblance to hay.

Arabia has been described as one of the driest, least hospitable deserts where temperatures can ordinarily reach 114 degrees Fahrenheit[1] and, on occasion, approach 130 degrees Fahrenheit.[2] Dust storms are hazardous to Arabia as snowstorms are hazardous to North America. During my months in Arabia, I experienced firsthand the threat of a dust storm. Suddenly, people started closing doors, pulling down windows, and stuffing rags in the cracks around door frames. We were sealed safely inside. It sounded like the roar of high winds as we sweltered in our airless cocoon. It was stiflingly hot, but thankfully, it didn't last too long. Emerging from the storm there was a sort of freshness, as if the sand had cooled the air.

We reached the hospital in darkness at around ten o'clock, and the lights powered by a generator welcomed me. The heat of the day lingered in the night air, and I was ushered into a two-bedroom prefabricated house. A desert cooler (a system that dampens the heat by the evaporation of water) greeted me with a breath of cool air. My hosts explained that the generator was normally shut down at ten o'clock, but as special dispensation for my arrival, it would be switched off at eleven o'clock and routinely turned back on at five o'clock in the morning. I had enough time to orientate myself to my new abode before lights out.

The water that came out of the faucet was scalding hot, too hot to hold your hand under. A bathtub had

---

[1] 45 degrees Celsius
[2] 54 degrees Celsius

been filled with a generous measure of water with time enough to cool before my arrival. I peeled my stockings off and plunged in. Luxuriating in the cool water and oblivious to time, the lights flicked off, the desert cooler stopped, and the hum of the generator silenced. My eyes adjusted; the light from the night sky was enough for me to make my way around. The heat clung to me like being wrapped in a thick fur coat in the summer sun.

Unable to sleep, I explored the house. The fridge had been well stocked with Coke. Not usually fond of the black fizzy pop, I guzzled its coolness. To my delight, I discovered an air conditioner and counted the hours until five o'clock, waiting for the generator to come back on and power it up.

They had told me it was safe to sleep outside. Not sleeping inside, I thought I would try. The stars in the Arabian sky were so bright it was just like daytime, and the moon was so beautiful. It felt cool enough to sleep, but the strange noises of the night frightened me back inside. The moaning and groaning, mingled with high-pitched bleats and low rumbling roars, was too much for me. Soon enough, I would learn to recognize ordinary camel noises, and the night sounds would become familiar and safe. The generator fired up, I switched the air conditioner on and slept until about ten o'clock.

With flip flops on, I picked my way across the hot sand to my host's home, burning my feet with every step. It was too hot to eat breakfast. We chatted politely for a while. Then, very gently, they explained that when an air-conditioner was turned on, there wasn't enough power for anything else. Crestfallen, the air-conditioner lay dormant for the remainder of my stay.

In that first week, I drank water, ate very little, and puffed and panted the short distance between my house and the hospital. The hospital was also a simple prefab building with a tin roof that housed an outpatient clinic and a delivery room. A straw building was erected alongside it, where the women would rest for a few days after a difficult delivery. (During my stay, this inpatient structure burned down. A cooking stove with an open flame had started the fire.)

A crowd gathered in anticipation of meeting the new doctor. Expecting a female doctor, they didn't trust me at first because I had short hair—they weren't sure whether I was a man or a woman. Dressing in a scrub dress didn't really help identify my gender either because culturally we dressed so differently. Women wore a mesh mask tied around their head. Initially, the ladies wouldn't even allow me to examine their throats. Through an interpreter, they would indicate a sore throat, but when I asked to look, they would stay hidden under their veil. At the outset, it was very frustrating, but it was also a lesson for me as I began to understand the predicament of women. They gradually gained confidence in my gender with time and the repeated assurances of my interpreter, Suleman.

The stack of patient cards on my desk was piled high, and I thought I wouldn't finish by tomorrow noon, even if I worked all night. It was a tough day that first day. The medicines had different names, and the local people did not know the drugs by the names that I knew them by. At first opportunity, I studied the medicine stock to make sense of what was available.

I learned to manage medical problems that I had never previously seen. It was a very challenging and growing time where I was stretched well beyond what I was familiar with. Some patients came to the clinic on donkeys, others arrived on camels.

One of the most interesting medical problems I came across was unique to women affected by a local custom. Late one night, a message came from the nurse-midwife that I was needed at the hospital. A woman giving birth was unable to deliver her baby.

As I approached, I asked, "What's the problem?"

"It's a salt case," she informed me. Initially I understood her to say, it was an "assault" case.

Either way, I was at a loss, so with some apprehension, I inquired, "I beg your pardon. Pass that by me again. A salt case? What's salt got to do with deliveries?"

Well, that was the beginning of my education! I discovered that salt was packed inside the vagina after childbirth to stop bleeding and infection. This treatment would continue for the first ten days postdelivery. I examined the patient. She was pushing, but she couldn't get the baby out past a mid-vaginal stricture, most likely caused by a prior salt treatment.

It was a very difficult situation, and I turned to the midwife for advice. She told me the doctor usually makes some incisions. I pondered and remembered reading about Dührssen's incisions: a set of three cuts made in the cervix if the opening was too small to facilitate delivery. But there was a risk of tearing and hemorrhaging. With no alternative, I sighed a prayer and made three cuts: one at ten o'clock, one at two o'clock, and one at six o'clock. A healthy baby was delivered with no excess bleeding!

Another problem with salt treatments was the scarring and narrowing of the cervix that produced many cases of retained menses. After giving birth, the woman's cycle would resume, but without evidence of any periods. The women would come to the hospital complaining of abdominal pain, their uterus palpably enlarged. I soon mastered the technique of inserting a needle inside the vagina to pierce the bulge. Puncturing the build-up of pressure that would occur after about five months of missed menses forced a sudden eruption that would shoot out and hit the wall behind me. It's difficult to imagine me moving that fast, but I was adept at jumping out of the way.

One day the registration clerk, a fellow Canadian, flipped up the little window between our two rooms and laughingly said, "This man has brought his camel in because he's been in a fight with another camel. What shall I do? He wants you to sew up his camel."

So, I flippantly said, "Well he can't get in here without having a name." And on I went with seeing my patients.

Later that day, Suleman (who called out the names and brought the patients in) was calling out for the next patient, "Muhammed, Muhammed, Muhammed. . ." Well, he couldn't find Muhammed.

The registration clerk flipped up the window again and said, "Oh, that's the name of the camel!" So, we went outside to find the camel. Well sure enough, there was the camel with a big gash in his lower lip. What to do? He was down on his haunches and hobbled. The camel was in so much distress that they couldn't keep his head still. That was a challenging problem.

I figured he wouldn't be any quieter putting local anesthesia in, so I would just tackle the stitches. A male nurse, who was also working in the hospital, prepared a tray with all that I needed to suture the camel's lip. The nurse and I worked together. I would take a swipe with the needle, and the camel would take a swipe at me, and we'd jump back. Somehow, we got him sewed up, and the camel's lip healed.

It must've been close to a month after that, that the man came back with his camel to give me a ride. It was during the clinic time, so in a scrub dress, I rode the camel named Muhammed.

Shortly after I arrived in the Buraimi Oasis, I was to be presented to the sheik as the new doctor. I was escorted to this formality by a fellow foreigner, Ray. He looked after the foreign workers at the hospital, managed the small community of local staff, and liaised with the sheik. Ray ensured that we were all fed and watered, the hospital was supplied with whatever was available, and that all was in order. The meeting took place in an elaborately carpeted tent. My heart was racing, and if it was possible to feel nervously sweaty in the desert heat, I'm sure that I was. As we entered together, I noticed the entourage lining the tent walls. I was the only woman. I wondered how many of them were bodyguards, ready to slice up any person who even vaguely intimidated their master.

We sat cross-legged on the floor. My colleague was beside me, and I sat in the same line as the sheik, facing him. The sheik didn't speak English and I didn't speak Arabic. When Ray introduced me, I recognized my name and peered out from beneath the scarf covering my head and nodded. The exchange was brief, and when Ray indicated, we took our leave. I can't really recollect the order of things that happened or the pomp and protocol, but I do remember the intimidation and knowing that I was the only woman in that tent.

Sometime later, I was urgently summoned to the home of the sheik. His black Cadillac pulled up at the hospital in a cloud of dust. I was told to grab my bag and come: the sheik's son was ill. Sensing the emergency, I willingly obliged, and the driver taxied me over the sand as fast as he could. I hung on whenever the car lost traction and we were airborne over the dunes.

Expecting the sheik's son to be unconscious, I was surprised to find him sitting calmly, waiting for my arrival. He was a young boy of about ten years. He had fainted in the heat of the day, playing too long in the sun. To not offend my host, I did my utmost to hold a straight-faced expression, in keeping with the tone in the palace. I carefully placed my stethoscope on the boy's chest and felt his forehead with the back of my hand. After advising rest and plenty of fluids, and reassuring them that he would fully recover, I was driven back to the hospital at a much gentler speed. During my stay in Arabia, the sheik presented me with a baby gazelle.

A cultural highlight of my brief stay in Arabia was the opportunity to attend a festival. It was possibly a celebration of Ramadan. Women were adorned in brilliant pink, jewelled clothing, albeit cloaked in the heavy black of their burkas and mesh-covered faces: faceless women, their identity hidden. As they danced and spun their bodies around, a flash of colour tumbled out. I delighted in the sword dancing and the sound of desert music: the percussion of animal-skin drums mixed with simple mouth instruments.

There was a delay in the return of the doctor and his wife who were home on leave. Asked to extend my stay at the hospital for two weeks, I negotiated another month of leave from my residency at West Suburban

Hospital to include a two-week passage home via the Holy Land.

Having said goodbye to Arabia and brushed the desert sand from my feet, I travelled on to walk in the footsteps of Jesus in the Holy Land. A journey that brought me the greatest joy: Bethlehem where He was born, and Nazareth where He grew up, the Jordan River where he was baptised, the Garden of Gethsemane where He agonized in prayer before His crucifixion, and the Garden Tomb where His body was laid. I floated in the Dead Sea and walked the stone-cobbled path where Christ had carried His cross; it was a great privilege to have walked that street, and it moved me deeply. The Garden of Gethsemane was a cool and colourful contrast to the arid landscape of that day. I felt close to my Lord in this tranquil place where I was overwhelmed by my imaginings of what He might have felt that day as He faced His death for me.

My travels also took me to Lebanon, Syria, and Damascus, flying home via Rome, Paris, and London. On a whirlwind tour, I viewed the iron work of the Eiffel Tower and soaked in as much of the Louvre as was possible in a few hours, including a long look at the Mona Lisa. In Vatican City, I gazed up in awe and amazement at the paintings on the ceiling of the Sistine Chapel; I will never forget that—it was absolutely fantastic!

In London, I met up with Dr. Hemwall. He too was homeward bound. He obliged my request to be shown around the city, and I was most intrigued by the wax museum. The figures were so lifelike, I half expected them to speak.

Back in Chicago, the remainder of my residency was quite mundane compared to the adventures of my three months in Arabia and abroad.

Arabia was a unique experience. It was there that I first became aware of the needs of Muslim women and girls, and I discovered a unique place for a female doctor to work. God revealed to me that he had chosen a special place for me to make a difference in the lives of women. In hindsight, my time there had begun to prepare me for the work I would later undertake in India. And so, it was a trip of preparation and training.

Going to Arabia at that time brought me out of my comfort zone. This short-term experience in a small hospital in Arabia in the summer of 1963 taught me how to treat animals in need as well as humans with mysterious diseases, of which I was completely ignorant. God was always with me. He brought my life's purpose into focus: the fifth memorial stone of God's grace in my life. He guided me to do something uncomfortable and showed me His unique design for my life.

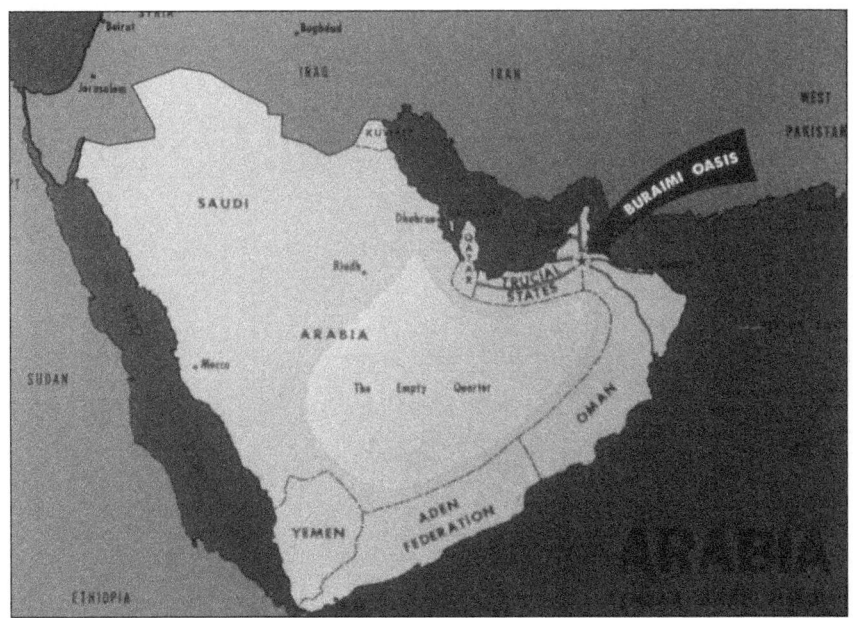

Map showing location of Buraimi Oasis 1963

Abu Dhabi Airport 1963

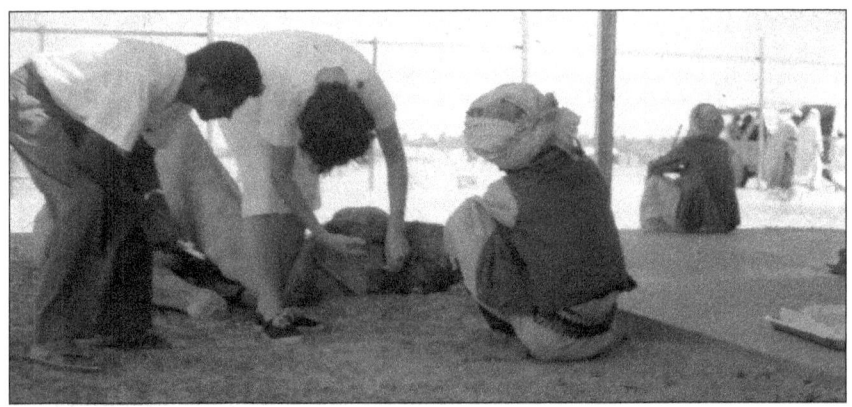
Dr. Bell sewing up camel's lip

Dr. Bell riding Muhammed

For this is how God loved the world: He gave his one and only Son, so that everyone who believes in him will not perish but have eternal life. God sent his Son into the world not to judge the world, but to save the world through him.

                                                John 3:16–17 (NLT)

FOREIGN FIELD

She was about eight years old. Her arm was burned beyond repair, and her tiny hand was gangrenous before she reached us. I cut away the destroyed tissue, and the nurses snuggly wrapped what remained in a stump bandage. Remembering her battle for life reawakens the anguish I staggered through back then. Only the Spirit of God could have sustained my faith: He shouldered the burden and the helplessness I felt.

Her name was फूलकली (Phulkali) meaning फूल की कली (flower bud). Her parents said she had fallen into the fire, or was it that her clothes burst into flames when she was making tea? Perhaps she was a child bride, and her family had been unable to meet the demands of her dowry. Whatever the cause, at least 50 percent of her skin was damaged: one leg, one arm, and her face spared. The burn was very deep, and the damage on her leg reached down to the bone. It was a miracle that she had survived.

It was a first for my eyes when Phulkali's urine came out green! Consulting my medical books, I discovered that a pseudomonas bacterial infection could cause green urine syndrome. She survived; I used the strongest antibiotic we had on hand. She was far from well, and her recovery depended on a blood transfusion. I gave a sample of her blood to her family.

"Take this to Lucknow," I instructed them. "Your daughter needs blood." (At sixty-eight miles[1] away, Lucknow was our closest city.) Several days later, they returned. The blood they brought back was contaminated: blooms of mould had sprouted, and the furry fungus growing inside the bottle made it unusable. Although the blood itself was spoiled, Phulkali's blood type was revealed, and to my delight, we shared the same, O positive.

We were not equipped to collect blood for transfusions, so I simply lay down on a bed beside Phulkali. Without a vacuum-sealed bottle, the nurses rigged a needle to one end of a long length of tubing and poked the other end into a sterile bottle, positioned on the floor. We relied on gravity—and my heart pumping—to collect a bottle of blood.

A lady from Switzerland, Elizabeth, fluent in the local language, wandered among the patients and their families, seeking to comfort them and to teach them about the Christian faith. Watching me give my own blood to Phulkali, Elizabeth shaped a story to illustrate salvation.

"You see the doctor giving her blood to save Phulkali's life?" she asked, then answered, "That's only her earthly life." Continuing, she explained, "Jesus Christ is God's son. Jesus was condemned to death for claiming to be

---

[1] 110 kilometres

the Son of God. He could have saved Himself, but He did not. Instead, He offered Himself as the perfect sacrifice. He gave *His blood* to save us. Salvation is God's gift. It is a gift of freedom from our sins." Patients and their families listened intently as I lay beside Phulkali, a doctor positioned on par with them.

Phulkali was a sweet little girl—so very brave—with a smile that embraced your heart. None of us escaped her warmth, and we were all very fond of her and devoted to her care. She needed nursing support to keep her clean and comfortable; one of the nurses would stay with her in the hospital each night. I marvelled at Phulkali's sparkle and bright countenance despite the great destruction of her body. Months passed, and she slowly, but surely, began to heal.

Medical supplies were a four-hour drive from Utraula. Every so often, we would make the journey for essential provisions. However, this one time, I regretted leaving my post. I had heard the grumblings going on in the background as her family was waiting for an opportunity to take her. Phulkali was of no value to a poor village family. With only one hand and her chest severely burned, she would have no means of breastfeeding a child of her own. Her womanhood ruined; her parents would not be able to arrange a marriage.

One day while we were away buying medical supplies, the family came to the hospital and demanded to take her home. Not recovered enough to survive out in the village, Phulkali's untimely death would surely come.

They had taken her home to die. Our little flower bud would never blossom. It broke our hearts.

Phulkali never did leave my heart, a scar of her suffering remains. She lived a little while longer, having shared my blood with her. But she died in the sickness of our world. I cling to the Lord's promise that "if we die with him, we will also live with him."[2] I hope and trust that Phulkali died in the arms of Jesus.

Working and living in the United States was another world, far distant from farm days in Canada. The comfort of life in Chicago was appealing, and it would have been easy to drift along. Arabia straightened out my attitude, and I remembered my beginnings: Trixie struggling for breath and a child-like bargain made with my Creator. My experience showed me that many people in developing nations did not receive basic health care and Muslim women did not have access to a female doctor, as they needed. The ongoing purpose of my life germinated and kept me searching for ways to serve Him as I had promised.

With my attention pulled toward the care of Muslim women, my first thought was Pakistan. India, although home to a plethora of religious beliefs, was known to me as a Hindu nation, so it did not make any sense to go there. Continuing to work at West Suburban Hospital, I met many interns who had immigrated from India. I

---

[2] 2 Timothy 2:11 (NLT)

asked them if they planned to go back, taking their skills to the people in their homeland. Shy smiles and an intriguing vagueness answered my direct, personal questions. Without knowing, I was beginning my relationship with India and its people.

Aspiring to work in a developing nation, I planned to join a charity with an interfaith Christian tenet. This charity would also need to offer health care in areas where my being a female doctor would be useful. While living and working in Chicago, I met an American couple, Peter and Cae, who were leaders in such a charity. They invited me to their home for meals and to spend the weekend with them whenever I was not working. It was a welcomed change, especially not having to eat hospital food that smelled and tasted like overcooked cabbage.

Peter and Cae were an older couple, around the same age as my parents. Their daughter Joy was a nurse, stationed on the outskirts of Utraula, in the northern Indian state of Uttar Pradesh. I was surprised to learn that it was a Muslim area. Although there was a government hospital in the city, it was difficult for women, children, and leprosy sufferers to access medical treatment. Husbands would not allow their wives and daughters to be seen by a male doctor, and people with leprosy were thought to be contagious and were cast out from society. Joy and her fellow workers prayed and asked God for a medical doctor to join them while, at the same time, Peter and Cae actively recruited me, making India sound appealing.

Historically, the charity rented a house in Utraula and opened a dispensary on the back veranda. In those days, a dispensary in India was a small-scale community outreach where basic medicines were given out and minor wounds were bandaged. People with leprosy started coming, but the workers were unfamiliar with how to manage this condition. At first, they bandaged the sores on their feet but then found the bandages hidden in bushes a short distance away.

One of the workers, Pearl, developed a deep compassion for the people who came to the dispensary with leprosy, and she desired to be of greater help to them. She placed herself under the tuition of an expatriate doctor who worked in a leprosy hospital in nearby Faizabad. Pearl learned to diagnose and treat leprosy with medication (dapsone and vitamins). However, fear of leprosy and stigma of the disease caused a local opposition to the work of the dispensary.

The sustainability of leprosy work in Utraula was discussed at the charity's monthly meeting in Gonda. Initially, not everyone was in favour of the endeavour, but following lengthy discussion, land was purchased about one mile[3] east of Utraula. The land comprised a guava orchard, and to my delight, mature mango trees, yielding sweet fruit in the monsoon season.

Pearl started the leprosy clinic with a table and chair under a guava tree. A building was constructed for the outpatient clinic, followed by a house where Pearl and other workers could live. After a time, another small

---

[3] 1.6 kilometres

building was constructed to accommodate two leprosy patients. Other workers, like Joy, joined the team working in Utraula. The charity recognized the need of basic health care for women and children in nearby villages and decided to act, but to proceed, they also recognized the need of a female doctor to join their team.

Peter and Cae encouraged me to pursue membership with the charity and join the team in Utraula, becoming the female doctor. God had been preparing me for this opportunity: He had taken me to Arabia and shown me the specific need of Muslim women; He had introduced me to Indian people living in Chicago. I had asked Him to show me where to go, and this was a neon-lit sign: Step This Way. My gut was certain. I knew that this was it, so I applied.

It was not long before I signed on with the charity for a long-term commitment. It is difficult to imagine these days, but back then, I signed on for the "length of my working days" (until retirement). The cycle of work and vacation would be five years working in India, followed by one year of vacation in North America. In addition to my doctoring, I joined the charity and the team in Utraula to oversee the building, equipping, and staffing of a hospital, primarily for women and children.

Despite my dad speaking Gaelic, I was monolingual, and I wondered how I would curl my tongue around a language so different from my own. All that I recall from my orientation before leaving North America was the satirical wisdom of the director of the charity who said, "Remember, *He* opened the mouth of the ass and she spoke!"[4] An encouragement for the language learning to come, reminding us of an account written in the Bible where God gave a donkey the ability to speak.

The passage to India took four weeks on a freighter ship across the North Atlantic Ocean, from New York to Bombay. A five-year supply of everything I imagined I would need was packed into barrels. It was difficult to figure out how many rolls of toilet paper to include in the stockpile! The voyage across the ocean was restful and refreshed me for what lay ahead. Although we were almost constantly surrounded by storms, the ocean beneath us was so quiet that the captain of the ship passed comment that *someone* must be praying. I quietly corrected him by putting it in the plural: that is, *many* people were praying.

We set sail October 30th, 1964; I was twenty-seven years young. Preparations for India had exhausted me. For the first five days, I slept. When I finally woke up, I enjoyed both the sights and the journey. It was good to relax and chill out. Travelling by freighter eliminated any jet lag, and the rest somehow lessened the jolt of arriving in another culture; everything seemed more manageable. My stomach churned a bit when it was empty, but it soon settled with a feed of breakfast. I enjoyed the tasty food served at the captain's table.

---

[4] Numbers 22:28 (KJV)

The *Hoegh Cliff* carried four passengers. One of the other passengers was a retired bachelor-lawyer from Washington. He hated women, doctors, do-gooders (and perhaps the whole human race)—so you know where I stood.

We reached Gibraltar following ten days at sea, and I felt just like Columbus discovering new-found land. I explored the Rock of Gibraltar through my binoculars and delighted in seeing dolphins jumping out of the water. The captain permitted me to "steer" the ship a couple of times. On these occasions, everyone clutched a life jacket, just in case. I was always on the bridge, ready to "help" guide the ship into port.

Unfortunately, my essential doctor's tools (stethoscope, ophthalmoscope, and auroscope, among other things) had been left behind in a New York taxi. On the day I had shipped out, aside from the goods loaded in barrels, I had carried with me numerous suitcases and other carry-on luggage. Included was a small suitcase acting as a travel-sturdy doctor's bag. An unseasoned traveller, I had neglected to count the pieces, and after wrestling the haul into my stateroom, I realized that one case was missing—the one with my medical equipment. The taxi had long since departed. I mourned my stupidity and grieved the sudden loss of my kit that was so crucial to my work.

The New Yorker who had helped me and my things to the harbour was not hopeful of retrieving the suitcase but promised to contact the taxi company and to pray (and ask others to pray) for its return. I had heard nothing before leaving New York. We docked in Tripoli, Libya for a few hours, but I did not go ashore. However, a message was waiting there. The taxi driver had found my suitcase in the trunk at the end of his shift and returned it to the office of the freighter company. They sent it out with the next ship, and I was to be reunited with my medical equipment in Bombay. God graciously answered our prayers.

Two days docked in Alexandria gave me the opportunity to disembark and explore this Egyptian city. I joined a driving tour that took me as far as Cairo. We drove through the Nile Delta and visited a magnificent mosque. Its interior a breathtaking display of the ancient, skilled craftsmanship in wood, ivory, alabaster, silver, and gold. Just outside Cairo, I eyeballed the Great Sphinx and the three big pyramids. The Egyptian Museum in Cairo contained the remains of Tutankhamun, a pharaoh encased in over 240 pounds[5] of pure gold! Imagine all that gold!

The Egyptian farmers tilled the soil with oxen and scattered seed by hand. I gazed in wonder at an ox and a camel yoked together pulling a wooden plow—what an odd combination. A water wheel used to irrigate the land with water from the Nile was driven by an ox. What a primitive way of life! The four-lane modern highway of 1964 between Alexandria and Cairo was cluttered with donkeys, mules, horses, camels, oxen, sheep,

---

[5] 110 kilograms

goats, and people. The sights began to prepare me for the ancient ways of India.

I re-embarked the freighter at Port Said where I glimpsed beggars—street dwellers and dirt were all that I could see there. We entered the Suez Canal and sailed through the Red Sea; every day it grew hotter and hotter. My body began to perspire, and I was thankful when the air-conditioning was turned on.

Finally, we arrived at Bombay Port Trust, the gateway to India. It was a busy port, and we waited out in the harbour for a long time; I cannot remember how many days we anchored there. Eventually, they disembarked the passengers and ferried us to shore in a small boat. The freighter followed in later when there was space for them to unload. Bill (a member of the charity I had joined) greeted me on the wharf. His pale face was easily spotted amid the crowd of dark skin tones, tanned deeper by their work under the sun.

He led me through the fish market. The stench of rotting fish and the stomach-turning sight of millions of flies blanketing them was ghastly! You could not see the fish until you were near enough to scatter the flies, just for a moment, with frantic hand flapping. I soon learned, and thereafter taught, that a bad sense of smell was one of the three prerequisites for travel to India. (The other two were a good sense of humour and a large quantity of patience.) A mass of people moved along the wharf, and the unrelenting cry of the fish mongers assaulted my ears. Not understanding the language of the port, their voices blended into a noisy din.

We stayed close by at a Salvation Army-run accommodation. The interior walls were painted a dark green that seemed to suck what little light leaked in from a few small windows set high up in the wall. The fishy smell permeated the air. I never wanted to go back to Bombay.

Relief came when my goods cleared customs and were loaded onto a freight train. Bill and I boarded a passenger train for our three-day journey to Basharatpur. Our carriage had three-tiered bunks made from hard wooden boards.

My eyes began to see poverty as I had never seen poverty before. Children were naked and dirty (not just grubby from play) but layered in the dust of the earth, the ash from open fires, and the garbage they rummaged through, searching for food. Their hair was matted, and their upper lips crusted with gunk from their noses. People squatted in the fields for lack of public conveniences. India imprinted her poverty and the sad faces of her people on me. Millions thronged the streets and plodded about their work despite frail bodies, malnutrition, and physical ailment.

Drought depleted the food supply, and the remnant of rice that remained was strictly rationed. The famine and hunger conditions of 1965 resulted in many people with specific diseases not responding to standard treatments. Later, when we placed them under our daily care and gave them regular meals, almost immediately, they began to improve.

The seasonal climate in North America had not prepared me for the seasonal climate in India. The contrast of cold to heat was extraordinary, and acclimatizing was perpetual—you never truly grew accustomed to the disparity between the continents. Although India was well-known for its intensely elevated temperatures, it was not always hot in North India; December through January offered a reprieve. A coldness briefly smothered the heat, and one drew comfort from a blazing fire and the closeness of blankets. Poor villagers died from cold exposure during these months for lack of firewood and warm clothing.

But when the fire of the sun scorched the earth, the thermometer regularly exceeded 100 degrees Fahrenheit.[6] With the added humidity, and no electricity to turn a ceiling fan, the heat quickly wilted your sense of humour and melted any patience you thought you possessed. Tempers flared and physical health declined. The heat became more oppressive and exhausted me each day.

During the monsoon, it was not unusual to see black fuzzy stuff growing in the bristles of my toothbrush—a douse with hydrogen peroxide quickly destroyed that fungus! One day the moisture was so heavy, water dripped from the ceiling in my office. I used an umbrella to keep dry. In the contrasting hot and dry months on

---

[6] 38 degrees Celsius

the plains in Utraula, I sometimes enjoyed "air-conditioning." I would hang a dripping-wet bath towel on a rope strung across my room. When electricity was available, the blades of the ceiling fan turned, evaporating the water and cooling the air.

The one advantage of the heat was the abundance of mangoes, a deliciously juicy fruit. While I enjoyed the mangoes, the staple food of the North was curry and rice. The warm spices laced with fresh hot chili pods singed my tongue and burned my gut, *all* the way through. The heat of the food lingered, and my system never fully adjusted to the cuisine.

People who have toured in remote or far-flung lands usually possess a collection of travel escapades. New and unfamiliar modes of transport offer interesting tales, but in India, even the familiar can be challenging. I never personally owned a car in India, but I did possess an Indian driving licence, an elaborately folded paper document written in Hindi script.

For short distances, I generally walked. The hazards included cows (who always had the right of way), the occasional torrent of water, and sticky black mud—all amid the masses of people. I learned to keep a steady pace and weave confidently through the bustle; it is more difficult to hit a moving target, so staying in motion was the best approach.

A cycle rickshaw was a reliable means of moving about and contributed to the local economy; although, negotiating an uninflated price could present a problem.

Roads were uneven and mostly torn up by weather and traffic. Carts drawn by horses offered bumpy rides. Horses were small and unkempt, and they seemed knock-kneed and hobbled—their loads often far too heavy for their frame.

Greater distances were traversed by bus or by train. Buses carried at least twice their designated capacity. A forty-passenger bus squeezed in eighty people (or more!) along with their luggage and the occasional livestock: a goat or a few chickens. The physical distance between seats was less than comfortable. Unless you were petite, you found your knees jammed up toward your chest.

Passenger overflow was balanced up on top, and the men with "low-class" tickets were responsible for push-starting the bus, should it be required. Roadside toilet breaks were exactly that! Men to one side of the road and women to the other. Timetables were a guide only. Trains offered a smoother experience, although equally crowded and grimy. Third class presented the most cramped and dirty space. (Ever needing to be frugal, I often travelled this way.)

Stopping at the stations, the sellers would bring through steaming kettles of मसाला चाय *(masala chai)*, spiced tea and coffee, with baskets of boiled eggs and other snacks for purchase. Small urchin children squatted and moved through the carriages, sweeping out the garbage with hand-held brooms. They paused along the way for payment of service, begging with a cupped hand and pleading eyes.

Language learning was a frustrating experience. Previously, I understood and used one language, English—it was as natural as learning to crawl, stand, and walk. Hindi is a phonetic language with more characters in its alphabet than English. The characters each have unique sounds. Some sounds are made with a puff of breath, and others are made by rolling your tongue backwards and pressing it to the top of your palate. It was an aerobic workout for my face, and I felt like Eliza Doolittle with a mouthful of marbles in *My Fair Lady*. Language study required a certain fortitude to hold myself to the daily hours of studying long vocabulary lists and grammatical rules. I learned the language by memorizing model sentences by heart.

Hindi was fundamentally taught from the हरी किताब (*haree kitaab*), green book. Textbook learning, we read stories and answered comprehension questions. Language school was in Landour, Mussoorie, historically built by the British Indian Army in the foothills of the Himalayas. It was a tranquil setting for learning. On a sunny day, we viewed the distant, white-blanketed mountains. The greenery and flowers were a welcome contrast to the drudgery of language study.

Small group-sessions in the mornings contained about six people, and the afternoons were allocated to private study and self-directed learning. I employed the help of a tutor. Aside from her, there was little opportunity to practice language. Eventually, when I did begin to work with village women, textbook Hindi had not prepared me for speaking and understanding local language. They were incredulous that a doctor spoke their language less fluently than their small children. It was a difficult period for me, a life lesson in humility.

At Landour Language School, students lived in group accommodations. I shared a room and a bathroom with three others. We celebrated American Independence Day on July 4th, 1965. For the celebration, we opened a big tin of ham. My contribution was to organize a series of games. It was a fun night! Later, asleep in our bunks, a grumble in my gut woke me in the early hours. That is when it started: diarrhea and vomiting. As the night wore on, I wore down, staggering to the bathroom. Nobody heard me, and I did not wake them. Strangely, living in community, I was the only one afflicted.

It was the beginning of a battle with chronic diarrhea; a barrage of investigations and all sorts of medications never solved that mystery. The sickness lingered and drained my energy—I never fully recovered. My weight dropped to less than one hundred pounds.[7] A picture of me taken at that time shows me wearing a saree with my cheek bones sticking out. Determined, I never stopped language school, making the daily trek up the hill to the classroom.

It was a policy of the charity to acquire language proficiency *before* being permitted to engage in the work of your profession. A two-year program included written and oral examinations. Once achieved, the

---

[7] forty-five kilograms

Right Hand of Fellowship was given: full membership granted, and you could go to work. Although the charity was registered as health and social work, their labourers were mostly nurses and other lay people. I was the first doctor to join this charity. As such, I negotiated my position before leaving North America.

Prior to my departure for India, my work-life balance was tipped in favour of work. In addition to my full-time residency program at West Suburban Hospital, I had my after-hours job with Dr. Hemwall in his private practice, and I was also responsible for the staff clinic at Moody Bible Institute, on call both day and night. Devoting myself to language study alone and suppressing my desire to practice medicine would have been totally disagreeable. For that reason, it had been decided that I could practice medicine in India while learning the language.

With no other doctors working with this charity in India, it had been arranged for me to be seconded to another charity (in the short term). While learning the language by way of a private tutor, I was to work with a female obstetrician and gynecologist in Lucknow (the capital of Uttar Pradesh). Unfortunately, this plan flopped before I embarked for India. A second plan was developed for me to stay in Basharatpur with Bill and Kay while waiting for language school to open in Landour. They were near to my age and had a spare room to accommodate me. While stationed in Basharatpur, I hired a language tutor and dabbled in a village dispensary.

My practice was very crude in the beginning, waiting for the bulk of my equipment to arrive from Bombay. I opened abscesses with a razor blade and cleaned out dirty ears with a bobby pin and an enema-bulb syringe. Thankfully, while at language school in Landour, I was able to take part in medical work. Every Saturday, a New Zealand surgeon allowed me to accompany him to Lehman Hospital in Herbertpur, forty-four miles[8] from Landour. It was a two-and-a-half-hour drive winding around the hills. We worked together in general surgery; I was able to keep my hand in, with procedures like hernia repairs and emergency appendectomies.

My first Christmas in India was delightful—although it did not really seem like Christmas to me as I very much missed gathering with my family and friends, enjoying the festive food, and attending Christmas programs at church. Nonetheless, two English nurses, who lived and worked in Khalilabad, joined us in Basharatpur. They brought me a gift: a set of glass bangles. The nurses squished my little finger flat against my thumb and jammed my elongated hands into the glass loops, eight to ten on each arm! Every movement jangled the bangles together. To some, the clatter was melodious and to others, an irritation. I enjoyed the colour and the sounds. I shared my music, playing thirty-three-inch records on the record player and speakers I had shipped with me to India.

---

[8] seventy kilometres

We shared food parcels from our respective homelands and had quite a feast. Plum pudding and Christmas cake appealed to my sweet tooth. One of the churches who supported me financially included decorations in a Christmas parcel: a big red stocking with my name on it, and a tiny tree trimmed with little red lights. The local Indian Christians celebrated with firecrackers booming from Christmas Eve until January 2nd of the following year.

On breaks from language school, I visited health clinics and other non-government hospitals. Taking part in medical work was enjoyable but sad as I witnessed the sufferings of the people. I began to learn customs and beliefs that motivated the people and affected their health, and sometimes life itself.

A woman came with a breast abscess that responded to treatment with penicillin and drainage. She was nursing her first baby after eleven years of marriage. At four weeks old, her baby was very thin and unsettled. The woman struggled to breastfeed because of the abscess; however, her relatives assured us they were feeding her baby goat's milk. I examined the baby more closely, but I could not see any physical hindrance to keep her from suckling; the baby looked hungry. Then we discovered the problem: the baby was a girl. Unwanted by her father, she would only become a burden (needing money supplied for her marriage). Sadly, this neglect of female infants was commonplace. During that time, I also examined a three-year-old girl, weighing ten pounds.[9] She looked like a wizened babe in arms, except for her full set of teeth.

It was tedious and exceedingly difficult to settle down to language study when so much need for medical help surrounded me. My desire to start work in Utraula motivated me to push through the language requirement as fast as possible. I discovered that I could accelerate my learning through a concentrated study program at the cost of $200, the equivalent to one month's allowance. By October 1966, twelve months ahead of schedule, I completed my Hindi examinations, both oral and written. A huge weight lifted from my head!

Adjusting to life in a foreign land was challenging. Foregoing the familiarity of home, I slowly began to weave a life abroad. It stretched me and broadened my understanding of who I was and who God is, and the tapestry of my life grew more colourful than I ever imagined it would. Yet behind a curtain in my heart, I concealed a feeling of nostalgia, an unobtrusive longing for the sensations of home. But as the years passed, what was once foreign became familiar, and the intimacy of my homeland faded. My sense of belonging and affinity diverged. I began to understand the words spoken by Jesus, "Foxes have dens to live in, and birds have nests, but the Son of Man has no place even to lay his head."[10]

---

[9] 4.5 kilograms
[10] Matthew 8:20 (NLT)

Communications to and from India depended on "snail mail" and parcel post. I used Kodachrome film and had slides developed to send home. To accompany my slide show, I recorded a running commentary on audio tape. It would take three to four months to share about my life in this way. Frustratingly, letters were often opened and censored, so comments about the in-country problems I grappled with were kept to a minimum.

Paper maps, atlases, and world globes were mainstay navigation tools. Utraula was not marked on every printed map, and so only an approximate location could be communicated: thirty-two miles[11] northeast of Gonda. Correspondence was often an arduous task that I attended to either late at night or early in the morning. The mail service in India was often erratic; postal strikes and train strikes affected delivery. Regrettably, undelivered mail was occasionally destroyed by fire.

Sickness was an unwelcomed acquaintance in India. Bouts of malaria made me feel miserable, amid colds, fevers, and bacillary dysentery. Diarrhea and abdominal pain plagued my days, and sometimes I would succumb and take to my bed and rest. One time, a fever shot my body temperature up to 104 degrees Fahrenheit.[12] Without a doctor to consult, I self-diagnosed dengue fever, given my excruciating muscle and bone pain, severe headache, swollen neck glands, and a rash all

---

[11] fifty-one kilometres
[12] 40 degrees Celsius

over my body. It was late in August, monsoon weather with no air-conditioning. I felt so aggravated (perhaps cerebrally irritated with the infection) that I asked Eileen, the nurse who worked with me from the start in Utraula, to put a No Visitor sign on my door. I was beside myself.

In North America, working eighteen-hour days—without a break—for a lengthy period was not so difficult. However, it was physically very exhausting in the heat of India. Life in general was demanding and time consuming. Personal ablutions and laundry required upskilling and a little more effort. In the hotter months we bathed in a bucket. We drew water out of a bucket with a डिब्बा (*dibba*), a small container, and used it to pour water over our bodies. We drenched down, soaped up, and rinsed off. In the cooler months, we used an immersion coil heater to warm the bucket of water—I took a few unintentional shocks from that little device!

As for our clothes, my brother Milton had packed me off with a washing machine on the freighter. It did not last too well with the fluctuating surges of electricity. The local धोबी (*dhobi*), a man who earned money by washing clothes, stood knee deep in a water hole. He cleaned the clothes by beating them on a rough stone board and sloshing them around in the muddy, slimy water—no soap was applied. He spread the clothes out on the ground or a tree to bake them dry in the sun.

The fundamentals for comfort (but not considered essential) were plumbing with running water, flush toilets, and a reliable electricity supply. In Utraula, we were fortunate and thankful for four out of twenty-four hours of electrical power a day. In between, candles or kerosene lamps provided light, just like in the days of the pioneers. It was common to perform surgery by flashlight. Thankfully, in 1974, we were given a grant to install a generator.

Before the hospital in Utraula was built, setting up outpatient clinics was the beginning of the medical work there. Within months, more than one hundred patients overwhelmed the outpatient clinics every day. Unable to cope with all the women and children who came, we had to turn some away. There was too much work and too few staff. Many patients who came asked for an injection, associating a needle with a remedy. We obliged by giving vitamin injections. Whenever I was not sure about a patient's illness or disease, I gave them a handful of vitamins and asked them to come back the next day. That would give me time to consult my medical books and to try and figure out what was wrong with them.

When I first arrived in Utraula, I had been given the directive to build a hospital. Pearl transferred to work in Landour, effectively handing me the torch and enabling me to take up the responsibility for the work that she had developed. However, my arrival caused some challenges.

Following the sudden death of her husband in India, one of the older foreign women in our charity, Mrs. T., had remained working in Utraula to oversee day-to-day activities, like buying food and preparing meals. She originated from the generation before me and did not have any knowledge or understanding of the processes and procedures in medical practice. Inevitably, we struggled to appreciate each other's perspective, and this created some untenable times.

We, the younger folk, respectfully tolerated Mrs. T. Her reputation preceded her; she was known for her sharpness and for adhering to tradition despite extenuating circumstances. Being new, I kept the peace until one fatal day I loosened my tongue. It was Good Friday, and at that time, the tradition among Christians in India was to meet for three hours on the morning of Good Friday to pray. However, that day two or three bullock carts had brought sick patients in from the village.

Each new arrival caused a commotion, and one by one we medical staff slipped out of the prayer meeting to care for the sick. The patients' needs were critical. Hours passed as we worked, and we missed the noon meal. Mrs. T. was unimpressed by our absence from the prayer meeting. However, she expressed her contempt publicly and indirectly—it inflamed me.

I confronted her. The critically ill could not wait until after the prayer meeting. The conflict in prioritizing medical care over spiritual traditions abated, but it proved difficult for me to work under this tension. Soon after, Mrs. T. retired to her home country, and I was able to continue unhindered in my work. Had I been fettered by tradition, I would not have been able to remain in India.

In the Bible, I read about the earthly life of Jesus. I learned that He travelled and visited different villages and towns. He related with many diverse people. He instructed people about Himself, about life, and about his Heavenly Father. He urged people to love God. He also healed the sick. Jesus demonstrated care for the whole person. For me, to share my faith in Jesus was to allow His love to shine through in my helping people in both physical and spiritual hardship.

By November 1965, I began to establish my homebase and work in Utraula. I also inherited the responsibility of a leprosy clinic that had been established in a nearby village, Ikauna. (Pearl had started this clinic, making a weekly journey by bus). Ikauna was about thirty-five miles[13] from Utraula, but as the road was not good, it took about two hours by car to make the trip, one way. With no lavatory there, when you *had* to go, you squatted in a nearby farmer's field, hidden behind a mustard or a lentil crop, or around the other side of a tree!

We were just beginning to find out about the prevention and treatment of leprosy. Each month, we set ourselves up outside in a mango orchard with several wooden stools and an enamel bucket to catch the "debris." It had a lid. We used the same bucket all day—the flies were free! Amputated toes and

---

[13] fifty-six kilometres

sloughed-off tissue dropped in, and we took it all back home to Utraula to deal with. The refuse was thrown into an open pit where crows picked it over. Maggots cleaned up the remainder. We advanced when we set up an incinerator for medical waste.

One fellow, who never came regularly, as he should have, consequently developed yet another gangrenous toe, the last one remaining on that foot. He calmly watched the whole procedure and, with a flippant wave of his hand, said, "Oh, whatever she wishes, she takes off." I always exhibited the amputated toes, holding them up with forceps.

We gave patients custom-made sandals to wear to protect their numb feet from further injury, but they never seemed to comprehend that it was a combination of disease *and* a lack of foot care that resulted in infection and consequent loss of toes. There was an acceptance of the disease and an expectation that toes would drop off. To please us, they carried their sandals to the clinic in their hands and put them on their feet to demonstrate their wearing of them. Some patients travelled long distances to hide the knowledge of their disease from their home places so that nobody would see them seeking treatment.

As the clinic population increased, we stayed overnight at the local rest house in the village. It was not exactly wholesome accommodation, with no window, no water, and no toilet. It was a room with a roof. Several years later, I was able to negotiate the acquisition of land in Ikauna and supervise the building of a clinic. Land had been promised, but no one had followed up on the offer, so the transaction was not completed until 1970. When construction finally began, I supervised the building project, driving to Ikauna at least one day every week.

Eventually, leprosy became less prevalent with the advance of a multi-drug treatment. The work we had been doing was given over to a leprosy worker who would go out on his motorbike each day and distribute medicine. Some leprosy patients were engaged to help package the medicine. They were what we referred to as "burnt-out" leprosy patients, having had the full course of treatment, they would continue with regular medication for the rest of their life.

Long before my arrival, an Indian nurse-midwife prayed to God for the needs of her people in Utraula. A small collection of foreigners arrived and began a Christian outreach, identifying the physical needs of the people. Untrained but compassionate, they bandaged the wounds of leprosy sufferers' feet. They too began praying for the needs of the people in Utraula. God heard their prayers and guided me toward India. At the same time, He also led Eileen, a nurse-midwife from England.

Gulam and Sabir, long-term leprosy sufferers cast out by their own families, welcomed our arrival. As fellow believers in Jesus, our brothers shared the vision to build a hospital for their community. Gulam guarded our home and our work as our चौकीदार (*chokidar*), security guard. And Sabir worked beside us, dressing and bandaging the wounds of leprosy patients. Along with Jesus, the four of us banded together to build Prem Sewa Hospital.

It began with a general clinic building, which contained an examination room, procedure room, laboratory, pharmacy, and record room. Expanding from there, we built an operating room with an attached eight-bed ward. We commissioned a local builder and his team, as well as a fellow foreign worker, Milton, to supervise the construction.

Milton, my brother's namesake, lived in Gonda with his wife. One time, as I was beginning to reverse out of his driveway, Milton noticed a deflated tire. Examining it, he asked me, "Have you got a rubber band?"

"A rubber band?" I quizzed, not knowing what he was talking about. He shuffled around in his pockets, found a rubber band, and used it to secure the leaking valve. Milton was handy that way!

I was responsible for the blueprint and design of the structure as well as the acquisition and installment of the equipment. People from our home countries sent money, and their donations paid for the materials and building of the hospital. I managed the finances, but not without strain as money matters were not my strong suit. We began building without enough money to finish. With the walls built, more money came to build the roof. With the roof finished, more money came for the windows and doors. It was a day-by-day, piece-by-piece construction.

The Prem Sewa Hospital in Utraula for women, children, and leprosy sufferers of the area, officially opened in 1966. It was only days before that I finished painting the last window. Many Indian officials were invited to attend the ceremony. Alongside a selection of Indian treats, we served मसालाचाय (*masala chai*), spiced tea: a loose-leaf tea boiled with aromatic spices, together with buffalo milk and sugar. The hot brown brew was strained through a cloth for serving.

On the very morning of opening day, I jammed and slashed open my finger while setting up a surgical table. Not brave enough to suture the deep cut myself, I supervised Eileen to help me. The name chosen for the hospital, प्रेम सेवा (*Prem Sewa*), Loving Service, was sometimes more service than it was love when we became too busy, but the idea was that God would give us the strength to have both.

Equipping the hospital required some travel. One time, my fellow worker Milton accompanied me on the journey to Gonda to pick up an operating-room table. On our return to Utraula, we faced a riot across our path. A spate of student uprisings was occurring across India, attracting international attention. Despite our living and working in a rural area, we discovered we were not exempt from the unrest.

We came across two buses, their windows smashed and broken. The passengers reported the violence in the next village where students were throwing small rocks at passing traffic. We decided to proceed. Not too far ahead, we came upon about two hundred students blocking the road and brandishing hefty sticks. We stopped, and a handful of students approached the vehicle. We spoke with them, and they allowed us to pass through, unharmed. The following day, news reached us that two of these young students had been killed and ten officials injured. We thanked God for His protection in the ordinary work of our days and unexpected events.

Burns were more common in the wintertime, with fires kept burning just in front of village huts, which were constructed from bamboo, straw, mud, and cow dung. Mostly, it was the children who suffered burns. In February 1969, a family brought their baby, about six months old, to the hospital. His family told us that he had fallen off his mother's knee and rolled into the fire. At least 30 percent of this baby's skin had been damaged. Examining him, I decided that he would need skin grafting.

"Tell them to take the baby to Lucknow," I instructed the nurses.

An Australian nurse, Maureen, who had joined the team in the early months of 1968 to cover Eileen's leave, approached me and said, "You know they won't go there because they're too poor, and the baby will die."

Sadly, I agreed, but what could I do? Skin grafting required skills and equipment. How could I give a six-month-old baby a general anaesthetic *and* do a skin graft?

Not giving up, Maureen ventured, "I'll give the anaesthetic."

I responded, "Well, I don't have a skin grafting knife."

She left me. An hour later she returned, holding up a handmade skin grafting knife. "Will this do?" Her voice was determined and provoked me to accept the blade, and use it. Her eyes brimmed with a fiery compassion. She did not want to give up on this baby. With a pair of scissors and a hammer, she had chopped up a tin Band-Aid box and made a holder for a double-sided razor blade—Aussie nurses worked outside of the box, able to make do with what they had.

Maureen handed me the knife. "Well," I pondered, "they will not go anywhere else." So, I prayed, *Lord, help me with this!* We grafted the skin, and God healed the wounds. Miraculously, the baby did not get infected. The skin graft took 85 percent, and the baby recovered.

A baby remained nameless until at least one year of age, mainly because surviving infancy was so hazardous in the villages. Maureen, who adored all children, named the miracle baby Freddy. I never asked Maureen if she knew how to give an anaesthetic. Later, she told me she had just winged it!

Life in Uttar Pradesh was sometimes colourful. Weddings were lavishly celebrated in India and always generated great excitement in the community. An elephant, a long-standing symbol of good luck, was the transportation of choice for the groom. A wedding in

Utraula offered me my first ride on an elephant. With some trepidation, I seated myself on its back. When the elephant lurched and wobbled from kneeling to standing, I held my breath! Once her four huge feet were planted, I laughed with a mixture of delight and relief. Not loosening my grip on the ropes, I settled in and enjoyed the slow pendulous ride.

Finding time in Utraula to take a break from work was difficult. The intense heat and fourteen-hour long days often flattened me and caused me to feel weak, useless, and sick. At thirty-two years of age, my body felt at least sixty years old and ready for retirement. Illness sometimes enforced rest, and when I could not lift my head from the pillow, I stopped work. However, vacations in Kashmir truly refreshed me. Trekking in the Himalayan Mountains and sitting beside the fast-flowing streams and rivers, I could recover from endless days of heat and toil.

God's creativity and design was so awesomely displayed in His mountain landscape. My spirit quietened, and I released my problems and worries: they fell into the rushing water and were carried far from me into the valley below. I thank and worship God for creating such a beautiful place for His pleasure, as well as ours. At an elevation of 8,990 feet,[14] the air was fresh and cool. An abundance of lush vegetation, trees, and exotic flowers filled my eyes and heart with wonder. It was an

---

[14] 2,740 metres

awesome display and reminder to me of His magnificence.

We camped at Pahalgam, nestled in a pine forest adjacent to the Lidder River, with spectacular views of lofty snow-capped mountains. Pahalgam is a 930-mile[15] road trip from Utraula. It was a long, bumpy drive. One time, Maureen and I drove up in the Volkswagen Kombi we used as an ambulance. Exhausted and eager to arrive in the cool mountain air, I pressed on as the sun sank and night fell.

We continued on a section of road that tunnels straight through the mountain, known as Banihal Pass. It immediately connects you with the stunning nature of Kashmir and its cool, sweet-scented air. Darkness has a way of smoothing out the road ahead, that is, until a wheel plunges into a pothole and bounces you off your seat. We hit something not too far from where we stopped for the night, on the cool side of the mountain.

The next morning, it was Maureen's turn to drive. She drove at a lumbering pace, slowly winding the Volkswagen Kombi up the hills. A long line of traffic backed up behind us. Impatient, I questioned her ability to drive. Annoyed with my remark, she pulled off the road and parked. The engine was mounted at the back. Looking it over, to my amazement, I discovered that the metal bracket holding it in place had cracked and broken. The engine had dropped down and was swinging like a loose tooth.

---

[15] 1,500 kilometres

Maureen joined me, and we both stood staring pathetically at our predicament. As it happened, a passing military truck stopped to help. After several hours inspecting the problem and deciding what to do, the men jacked up the engine, drilled holes in the bracket, and secured it together with screws and heavy gauge wire. And so, we were rescued by the Indian Army; their roadside fix enabled us to drive slowly on to Srinagar.

On one occasion visiting Kashmir, three of us ventured out on a three-day hike to walk on a glacier. Returning to camp on the third night, I felt really, *really* tired. I lay down in our tent, skipped the evening meal, and slept. I was woken with horrendous cramps, and the night was filled with diarrhea and vomiting.

Our toilet was at the backside of the tent, screened behind a canvas flap. The seat was made of wood, and the bowl was a bucket slotted in underneath. That was one of the times I thought dying was my only relief. Maureen and Eileen identified my dire need for help. They also understood my resistance to being the recipient of medical care. Without a word, they walked me down the side of the mountain, one on each side. They bundled me into a taxi and took me to a hospital in Anantnag, where I stayed for about a week.

Our Volkswagen Kombi was in very poor condition; every time we drove it, we wondered if it would deliver us to our destination. The dust and terrible road conditions prematurely aged the motor—and any other movable part. It began to guzzle oil, and at the time, oil was difficult to buy in India. So, we applied for a permit from the Indian government to import a new motor, and we prayed for the funds to buy one. In the meantime, we nursed the old motor along.

Car troubles anywhere are inevitable, but in the boondocks of India, travelling in remote village areas, the nearest mechanical help could be miles away. With no roadside assistance, my range of practical skills developed. One of the nurses and I were driving home from the Ikauna clinic back to Utraula, when we realized we had a flat tire. Already worn out from the day, our first attempt to unscrew the rust-welded lug nuts failed. The X-shaped wrench did not budge any of them. We applied some oil and prayed. We heaved again, and one by one the lug nuts released their grip. With the spare tire successfully in position, we made it home.

Eventually, the Volkswagen Kombi met its demise, and a replacement became paramount. In the northern hemisphere summer of 1968, I relinquished my much-awaited annual vacation in Kashmir. Although my first five-year cycle was not yet complete, the charity gave me two-months leave of absence to travel home to Canada. The main purpose was to raise funds for a new ambulance. In return, I agreed to remain in Utraula until another doctor could relieve me before my full twelve-month leave. It would be my first airplane trip home since arriving in Bombay by boat in 1964.

With a short timetable, arranging speaking engagements was limited to whatever was possible. Opportunity to address the people in my brother Milton's church was during a midweek service. My sister-in-law Jean was bothered because the church did not pass a plate around for collecting any monetary offerings from the people at that gathering.

"That's okay," I reassured her. "It will be good to connect with people."

I gave my slide presentation. You can tell when your audience is with you and understanding what you are telling them. As I was speaking, I could see ripples of perplexed expressions. They did not have a clue what I was talking about. When I realized that Hindi words were hanging in the air between us, I scrambled to find their English equivalents.

At the end of my presentation, the pastor got up and said, "I know that nobody has come prepared to give any money in support of your cause tonight, but we are going to sit a plate at the back of the church, and any money collected will help buy this vehicle. Surely, we could put enough money together to buy a wheel or something."

When Milton and Jean took me to the airport, he asked, "Well, guess how much money you got?"

"I have no idea," I answered.

"You got $500! And, on top of that, they have decided to send you $25 a month!" I was speechless. Five hundred dollars was the equivalent of two and a half months' allowance. The whirlwind two-month trip home had successfully raised enough money for a new ambulance.

The most important lesson from Jesus was to love God with everything you are and have. The second most important lesson from Jesus was to love the people around you, unselfishly and without reserve, as you would love yourself. God placed a very deep desire within me to love and help people around me. People came to Prem Sewa Hospital with expressions of hopelessness. Being a physician, all I could do to love them was to listen and respond.

In India, a foreign field, the germination of my life's purpose had taken root. My heart, although weary and broken, was now fixed in this land of hardships and contradictions. Having poured myself into the work at hand, I realized my strength was not enough, the need was unrelenting. My body was tired and I ached for rest; however, God's presence, so evidently with me in the foreign field, is counted as the sixth memorial stone of God's grace in my life. Having directed my feet, He gave me courage to serve Him in a land far from my earthly home.

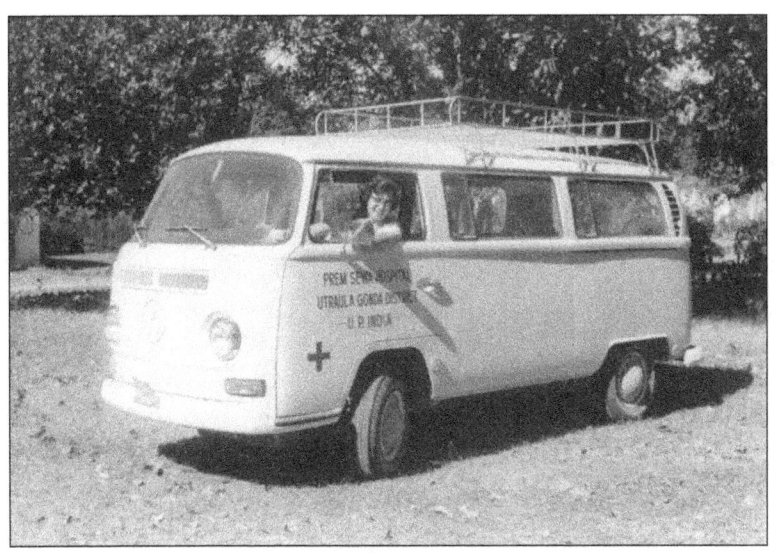

Dr. Bell driving Prem Sewa Hospital vehicle, Utraula

Sister M. Costello, Dr. A.G. Bell, MD, Sister E. Coates, Mrs. Raziya Begam, Mrs. R. Charles, Mrs. Shaida Begam, Gulam Masih, Sabir Masih

STAFF PHOTO 1969
Utraula, Uttar Pradesh, India

Dr. Bell standing near a field behind Prem Sewa Hospital

TWELVE STONES OF GRACE

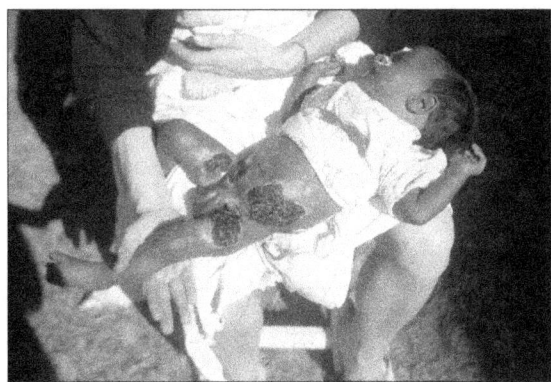

"Freddy" – burns baby Dr. Bell skin grafted with skin grafting knife Maureen made.

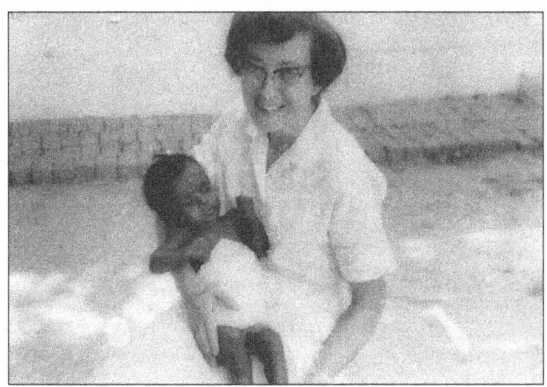

Dr. Bell holding "Freddy" after skin grafting

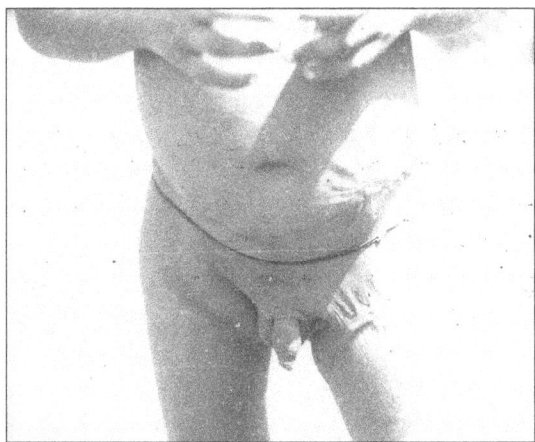

Skin graft healed!

Then Jesus said, "Let's go off by ourselves to a quiet place and rest awhile." He said this because there were so many people coming and going that Jesus and his apostles didn't even have time to eat.

Mark 6:31 (NLT)

FREEDOM

On our flight from India to Iran, we had a short stopover in Kuwait. Maureen and I sheltered in the air-conditioned transit lounge while our luggage transferred to the next flight. A problem transpired, and ground staff herded us outside; we lined up for a security check and identified our suitcases. It was at least 120 degrees Fahrenheit[1] with a blistering hot desert wind. The sole of my चप्पलें (*chappals*), sandals, slid over the molten, sticky tarmac. Clutching our hand luggage, we gasped in the heat like fish stranded on land. When we boarded the airplane, we expected the welcome of refrigerated air, but instead, we sat for an entire hour in an airless cabin—the engines lay idle to conserve fuel. This short leg of the journey did not include refreshments.

When I left Utraula with Maureen in July 1972, she was passenger in the red Chevy Van. I pressed hard on the accelerator, leaving a long trail of dust behind us. Maureen, who had never intended to stay in India long-term, bawled her eyes out! Incredulous, I asked,

---

[1] 49 degrees Celsius

"What in the world is the matter with you?" I could not understand her reaction because a ten-ton weight had lifted off my shoulders and I just wanted to shout, "Yippee! We are out of here!" I was singing and happy.

But Maureen, broken-hearted with the prospect of never being able to return to Utraula, said, "It's alright for you, you're coming back, but I may never see these people again!" I kept quiet. Seven years and seven months of striving and strain had exhausted me. Physically worn out, mentally fatigued, and spiritually deflated, there was nothing left. I set my gaze on the road ahead and concealed the private thought that I was never coming back. Not one glance in the rear-view mirror.

Back in Utraula, there was only one of me, and the work often extended into long stretches of the night. Drained by the endless days of work in the hospital and outpatient clinics, the चपरासी (*chaprasi*), messenger, often woke me for complicated childbirths. Initially, there were no overnight staff to take care of the patients who stayed in the hospital. If I had an intravenous running at night, then I had to have somebody there to manage it—and that somebody was sometimes me. I took my turn as night-duty nurse for patients who needed care.

Regardless of sleep, outpatient clinics started at eight o'clock in the morning. At lunchtime, during the hottest hours of the day, we took a two-hour break. If there were no other emergencies, I would go to the upstairs veranda and sleep. The outpatient clinics continued in the afternoon, and any patients not registered by five o'clock had to wait until the next day. There was an endless crowd of patients; I could never reach the end of the line—there was always another one to see.

Bookkeeping had also been my job, and evenings were frustrated by not being able to balance the books. In those days, I used a big ledger book to keep financial records, and the money that we collected was in a cash box. I am not even sure if I had a calculator—it felt like all I had were my fingers and toes! One advantage was that the recordkeeping was in English, so at least I did not have to struggle through in Hindi: १,२,३,४,५. . . (*ek, do, teen, chaar, paanch*. . .). One time, I was ₹1,000[2] short in the cash box, and I did not have ₹1,000 to replace the missing amount. I remember checking over the figures repeatedly, but I could not reconcile the missing money. Doing medical stuff was enough for me to manage without the added pressure of treasury.

Correspondence first reached India in February 1970 with news of a female doctor coming from Germany to relieve me in Utraula. Having joined our charity, she would ultimately arrive in India in August 1971 (eighteen months later!), along with her husband and her two young daughters. A replacement had finally come.

---

[2] one thousand Indian rupees

Dr. Maria and her husband, Stefan, were a welcome sight. Stefan occupied himself installing a new air horn on the Volkswagen, an essential tool for driving in India. It had such a high pitch that even the cows galloped off the road! Stefan was impressed by the large amount of work waiting for him. While he busied himself with maintenance, Dr. Maria accompanied me in the hospital and outpatient clinic every day; it was her first glimpse of the people and the diseases and illnesses prevalent in the poor villages around us. Dr. Maria and Stefan stayed in Utraula for one week before disappearing to language school, later returning to Utraula at Christmas (of 1971) to make their permanent base there. Too tired to express my gladness at their return, I smiled faintly and breathed a sigh of relief.

From Dr. Maria's initial arrival in India, I waited almost another twelve months for her to attend language school, familiarize herself with the work, and be equipped and ready to relieve my position. While I waited, an idea seeded: an overland trip in a Volkswagen Camper! The very thought energized me and kept me going. The Lord knew that I needed rest, and in the adventure of travel I would be able to completely abandon the pressures of my work. Motoring through landscapes and exploring the world would invigorate me and give me relaxed time and breathing space to gather myself.

In June 1971, I wrote a letter to my brother-in-law Harry (married to my sister Dorothy). Before automated teller machines, Harry managed my personal finances in Canada. In those days, banking was in person and records of deposits and withdrawals were handwritten into a little book.

I opened my letter to him with two questions:

> *Now Harry, how are your investments going? Are you interested in a new investment?*

I continued with a careful outlining of the facts:

> *When I depart India for my twelve-month leave, I would like to drive overland across Asia and Europe in a Volkswagen Camper. A friend has advised me that I can purchase a Volkswagen Camper at a 10 percent discount on the factory price direct from Germany. The total cost for the basic model would be $3,000, and for the same vehicle in Canada it would cost $4,500, so I would save $1,500.*
>
> *If I own the vehicle for one year before shipping it to Canada and keep it for another year before I sell it in Canada, I will not have to pay any custom duty either. Volkswagen has a good resale value in North America, and I think I would recoup the money spent. I have a couple of friends interested in making the trip with me so that will help to pay the travelling expenses.*
>
> *Now the problem is that I do not have enough money to buy the camper. Would you be willing and able to lend me $3,000? Being quite ignorant of things in Canada*

now, what would be the rate of interest? While I am home on leave, I could soon pay you back once I start working.

Suffice to say, Harry did not hesitate to "invest" $3,000 for me to buy the Volkswagen Camper. Excitedly, I sent a mail order to Germany. It would be months before it was ready, and with war between India and Pakistan brewing, I was hesitant to have the camper shipped to Bombay; however, I did not know an alternative. So, the camper shipped to Bombay, where I had first set foot in India seven years earlier.

Unfortunately, when I arrived at the port to receive the shipment, I discovered that I could *not* import the camper into India. The camper was stranded at sea on the freighter. By that time, the Indo–Pakistani war of 1971 had erupted, and there were increasing tensions between Iran and Iraq. Not knowing what to do, I visited colleagues stationed in Bombay to discuss my dilemma with them. Together, we decided to ship the camper to Iran where I could drive relatively safely by avoiding any simmering war zones. Armed with a plan, I returned to the port and arranged for the reshipping. That gave me about six months to make my way to Iran to collect it.

Much later, I realized that I did not even consider the depreciation on the vehicle, or that I drove the camper without any insurance! My brother Gordon alerted me to these things and told me that if anything had happened to the camper, I would not have been able to pay for it. (I never really put my faith and trust in the world system.) As it turned out, I was able to work when I arrived back home in Canada and reimbursed the money to Harry. About ten years later, I sold the camper for just over $3,000.

Maureen travelled with me on our overland trip all the way from India to Canada.[3] Maureen was the navigator. She could read a map and intuitively seemed to know what direction we were travelling, that was particularly helpful for when we had no map! Roadblocks, potholes, and inclement weather did not faze her, and whatever predicament we found ourselves in, she navigated through it with her Aussie determination and wit.

When we left Utraula, we drove to Delhi via Agra and watched the sun rise over the Taj Mahal, the warm orange glow reflected off the ivory-white marble of the tomb. From Delhi, we flew via Kuwait to Iran to collect the camper. When we arrived in Iran, the terminal that greeted us was a tin shed, causing Maureen to crumple onto the floor and declare, "I'm going to die right here!" Admittedly, the desert heat had almost consumed us in our travels. That evening, Maureen and I were cooling down in an air-conditioned room when she decided that she might just stay there until winter. We all have our limits; nevertheless, she continued the journey with me.

---

[3] Link to a Google Map of the 1972 overland trip, mapped using Dr. Bell's travel diary as a guide. Diary excerpts are embedded in the Google Map: https://www.google.com/maps/d/edit?mid=1D5cpNIXMtcXW4EnNDiEiF1x-CRoL81Xz&usp=sharing

Having arrived in Abadan, Iran, our air luggage took three or four more days to clear customs. We made our way to Bandar Shahpur[4]—a port city on the Persian Gulf. There was no key available to collect the camper, and so we returned the following day. Aside from a dead battery, the Volkswagen Camper was in good condition. Neighbourhood kids punctured a rear tire within the first few hours of it parked in the street. It cost 120 Iranian tomans to repair the puncture.

Our first day on the road was extremely hot; we kept ourselves covered in wet towels. The treeless landscape offered us no shade. Fortunately, we found shelter in a cave for morning tea. We travelled to Shiraz and explored palaces, mosques, and tombs of kings. We reached Tehran late at night.

Travelling by night was cooler, but as we discovered, also fraught with danger. Oncoming trucks turned off their headlights, forcing us to move out of their way. The road seemed to narrow in the darkness as trucks swept around the bends in the middle. It was difficult to pull off the road with deep concrete drains and gullies ready to engulf us. We had a near miss as one truck very nearly hit us—it was terrifying.

As planned, we picked up three travelling companions in Tehran. An English lady, a young German lad, and an American nurse. Five nations together in one Volkswagen Camper: Canada, Australia, England, Germany, and the United States. Keeping peace in the family was sometimes challenging!

---

[4] Now known as Bander Khomeini.

The English lady was a chaperone for the young German lad, Wolf. They both travelled with us for two weeks, as far as Ankara, the capital of Turkey,[5] before I took them to the airport (as arranged). Wolf was the son of a couple I knew from our charity. He had finished his school year in India and was returning home to Germany for summer vacation. Wolf's travel companion, the English lady, was a friend of his parents; I knew little about her. The American nurse travelled with us much further, but she too left us before the journey's end. I had met her at language school in Landour, and though she had been fun to be around, the close quarters of our overland trip dampened her frivolity and clouded our days.

We shared expenses for gas, oil, check-ups for the camper, and food (if we all ate together). The five of us camped in interesting places along the way. One evening, we pulled up for the night in the construction site of an exclusive yacht club, north of Tehran, where we took advantage of the toilet facilities and running water. Not too far from there, we camped in a beautiful grove of trees overlooking the Caspian Sea (near Ramsar, Iran) on the edge of a rich man's property. Another night, we set up camp in a clay-brick manufacturing site on the coast of the Black Sea, it was about twenty-five miles[6] from Rize, Turkey.

We delighted in the mountainous landscape, bursting with wildflowers—yellow daisies, roses, Jacob's ladders,

---

[5] Now Türkiye
[6] forty kilometres

and bellflowers. We picked wild blackberries for supper and enjoyed a late swim in the sea. A group of drunken men discovered our camp. The young Turks made interesting offers, but the presence of our young German companion proved to be good security. On our way to Ankara, we caught the tail end of a flash flood. Swirling mud and water gushed across the mountain road in front of us. Cars had stopped ahead and pulled us up out of harm's way. Thankfully, the torrent subsided before it reached us, and we made it safely through the deluge.

Maureen reminded me that she gave up one of her dresses to make me a pair of shorts. Shorts in rural India were taboo, and dressing appropriately for Indian culture was not always comfortable. So, on vacation, travelling through hot countries (where females wearing shorts was deemed socially appropriate), I was grateful for the provision. However, when she first presented them to me, I thought to myself, *Did she make these out of an old curtain? What a wild floral print!* But I soon learned that she had made them from one of her dresses. They were easy to wear and cool. That was until we reached Greece, when I ventured out into a field for a roadside pee. Without realizing the danger, I squatted down and brushed my backside on a cactus bush—the barbs hooked into my skin like tiny fishhooks. Armed with a pair of tweezers, Maureen spent the rest of the trip fishing them out!

Our travels in Greece took us through places I knew Paul the Apostle had once travelled; their names familiar to me from reading the Bible. In the first century, Paul's life work was to spread the Good News of Jesus' teachings. He wrote pastoral letters to the early churches, recorded in the New Testament portion of the Bible.

We wandered among the relics of an ancient theatre and tower in Philippi and marvelled at the Lion of Amphipolis on our way to Thessaloniki. In Athens, we rose before dawn to see the Acropolis, the highest point above the city, bathed in the sun's first light. We had positioned ourselves on Areopagus, also known as Mars Hill, to watch the sunrise over the ancient ruins. It was very impressive as we stood on the rocky outcrop, and for a moment, we stood immersed in Scripture.

It was here that Paul had once stood in the middle of Mars Hill and addressed the "Men of Athens," the Greek philosophers and others who had gathered there to listen. Paul spoke of the altars he had seen as he walked through Athens. He remarked that one of the altars had an inscription on it that read: *To an Unknown God,* and he explained that "this God, whom you worship without knowing, is the one I'm telling you about."[7] In the quiet of daybreak, we could almost hear the echo of Paul's words. Our spirits stirred within us.

Unintentionally, I had chosen a "hippie van" for our adventure. We came across other travellers with dented

---

[7] Acts 17:23 (NLT)

flowers, rust stains, and smudged peace signs decorating their Volkswagen Campers. When we arrived at country borders, it amused me to watch their vehicles searched from top to bottom. My camper was a shiny, new Sierra Yellow, and we were waved across with no problems.

Yugoslavia was under communist rule when we crossed the border. We had no difficulties entering the country, although the tension we felt crossing the border did not lift. It was normal to feel tension whenever we crossed from one country to another, as the muscle of border security always flexed. A sigh of relief usually followed as we passed through immigration and customs and drove into another nation, filled with the excitement and anticipation of exploring a new place. However, our arrival into former Yugoslavia and our travel there was unwelcomed.

Road signs were difficult to understand, and there were no road maps available. A map of 1972 Yugoslavia would be a vestige of history as the same journey today would take us through North Macedonia, Kosovo, Montenegro, Bosnia and Herzegovina, Croatia, and Slovenia.

If the weather was pleasant, we enjoyed our meal breaks outdoors. One day, we picked blackberries and plums and ate our lunch by the shore of a little inland lake. Another day, when we pulled off the road to eat our lunch, the police came and told us to move along—it was an unpleasant experience. Nevertheless, we enjoyed the beautiful mountain scenery, traversed winding roads of various qualities—from good to unbelievably bad—and drove through pouring rain. As we neared Austria, we glimpsed high snow-covered mountains and bought milk from people grazing sheep.

Austria was, by contrast, a friendly place. Whenever Maureen asked someone for local directions, the people would say, "Follow me!" and guide us to wherever we were going; they were very hospitable people. The mountain mist obscured our view from Grossglockner Pass—all we could see was snow! Unfortunately, we missed the fields of undulating green, carpeted with wildflowers, and the long view of the snaking road that wound its way forward and back on itself, where the mountain's edge was so steep. We could not see the high mountain slopes and shelves of rock piled with snow; the entire landscape was a whiteout! In Salzburg, we explored churches, castles, and cemeteries and watched a torchbearer arrive with the Olympic flame. (It was on its way to the Games of the XX Olympiad in Munich, Germany.)

We set foot in three countries: Austria, Liechtenstein, and Switzerland—all in one day! From Austria, we had a magnificent view of the Alps: the snow-laden mountains set against a blue sky. We crossed into Liechtenstein to glimpse the medieval castle in the capital, Vaduz, where the prince lived. It was like a fairy tale, with cylindrical towers and cone-shaped roofs reaching up to the sky. A breathtaking mountain scape framed the castle, with its walls scrolling high above the forest trees at its base. Such opulent beauty! Then, on to Switzerland, where we camped by a rushing stream.

In Interlaken, we visited the Swiss lady, Elizabeth, who had watched me give blood to Phulkali (the little girl severely burned in the village in India). Elizabeth had returned home to care for her aging sister. Their home was too small to accommodate us, so we slept in the camper, parked in a carpark just opposite. We had given Elizabeth's address to friends and family, so we were able to enjoy letters from our home countries and from our colleagues and friends in India.

From Elizabeth's, we drove to Lauterbrunnen and took the mountain cable car and electric train to Mürren. The mountain views were magnificent! In Switzerland, I remember seeing the cows and hearing the melodic bells buckled around their necks. Intrigued, I bought a small souvenir that now hangs on my apartment door to greet my comings and farewell my goings.

When we first arrived in Germany, we camped in the Black Forest and picked wild raspberries for supper. In Munich, Dr. Maria's parents hosted our stay and were anxious to hear news of their daughter and her family back in Utraula. Her mother spoke and understood a little English, so I was able to communicate something positive and reassuring. It was a luxury to have a hot bath and sleep in पक्का (*pakka*), absolutely first class and genuine beds.

The Olympic Games were in full swing, and the only tickets available were for the field hockey, so as not to miss the international event, we booked our seats. We cheered for Pakistan when they defeated Belgium 3–1. The next day, September 5th, we left Munich early in the morning for Hanover. That same early morning, a group of Palestinian terrorists stormed the Olympic Village. They shot and killed two Israeli athletes and took nine others hostage. All nine Israeli hostages died; eleven men murdered.

We were on the road when we first heard the broadcast. (That was before tape decks or CD players existed in vehicles, so we had the radio tuned for music.) Even now, as I remember that day, my stomach feels uneasy. Having been so near to the horror of what had transpired made it feel like we were right there. I guess proximity to human suffering can stir up intense empathy. The summer colours of the Netherlands washed over our shock. Like God's rainbow, the colours promised hope and a future.

Every ten years, an international horticultural exhibition takes place in the Netherlands called Floriade. In 1972, we were privileged to visit Floriade, which was being held in Amsterdam that year. We were counted as two of the four-and-a-half million visitors who visited the purpose-built site, Amstel Park. To my recollection, there was a profusion of flowers: clusters of uniform colours and geometric-shaped garden beds amass with tulips—red, orange, yellow, and pink. Roses bloomed in massive vases, with ponds of water swirling beneath them. The warm summer air carried the floral perfume.

It was a bee's paradise. What a wonderful way to immerse ourselves in all things Dutch.

In stormy weather, we crossed into Belgium without realizing it and had to backtrack to the Netherlands to mail our postcards already sealed with Dutch stamps. In Belgium, we visited Flanders Fields. It was overwhelming to see the number of graves from Commonwealth countries; "Row on row. . ." the familiar poem rang in my ears.[8] Pink and red roses adorned all the graves; the scent of their blooms filled the air.

Remembrance Day in Canada commemorates this battle every year, but it was not until I stood among the graves that I realized how vast war itself was. I had relatives who had fought in the Second World War—it made their experiences slightly more tangible for me. Although I knew one million soldiers were either wounded, missing, or killed in action in Flanders Fields, that number was meaningless until I saw the graves—even then, the reality was distant. I have not forgotten the realization of this loss of life and sacrifice, and I carry it with me to this day. Lest I forget.

We joined a bus tour of Paris, France, to explore the city. It was my second visit to the Louvre Museum, and I revelled in the detail of Rembrandt's paintings, enjoyed a second look at Leonardo da Vinci's Mona Lisa, admired the exquisite Greek sculptures, and marvelled at the ornate jewellery displays. The history of Notre Dame, the medieval Catholic cathedral, fascinated me—the

---

[8] Field, A.E. & McCrae, J. "In Flanders Fields," 1919.

site of Napoleon's coronation and of many royal weddings. From France, we ferried the camper across the English Channel to England and visited friends in Northern Ireland. We happily parted ways with our American travel companion somewhere in England.

When Maureen and I reached Scotland, we camped by the side of the road, overlooking a loch. We watched the sun sink over the water. The mountains, which were more like grass-covered hills, spread across the horizon. The ruins of a fort sat stoutly on the sandy shore. Low stone fences lined the fields in the sweeping hills around us. That evening, the water lay still, like glass—the little island in the middle of the loch held its reflection steady. Sunsets blanket the end of the day with calm, and although the night hides the sun, there is the promise of its return in the morning.

Knowing that Scotland was my heritage, I hankered to trace my roots on the Isle of Tiree, but just one boat made the crossing to the island, running only twice a week, and when we passed by that way, the days did not align in our favour. However, we came across white heather blooming in a field—the less common variety. Its rarity gives rise to it being a symbol of good luck. I carefully gathered a small piece of the tiny cluster of bell-shaped blossoms, cushioned it in wax paper, and pressed it between the leaves of a book. I later framed it and gave it to my dad. It reminded him of the homeland—a land that he had never set foot in (having been born in Canada), and yet he spoke its mother tongue.

I kept a lookout for the Loch Ness monster, but Nessie eluded my watchful eye. I did, however, delight in seeing the local fishermen cast their lines. The landscape of Scotland was so picturesque, and somehow, with my feet on the land of my ancestors, I felt strangely at home. My affection for animals was savoured by the highland cattle and black-faced sheep. Being out in the camper with the damp, rich smell of the earth, I was somehow invigorated.

Our overland trip ended when we shipped the camper across the North Atlantic Ocean to Montreal, Canada. It was an absolutely fantastic trip! An adventure that took me through sixteen countries and allowed me to explore landscapes from deserts to mountains to oceans.

Although the journey had refreshed me, my resolve to never return to India remained. It was onward to North America. At London Airport (Heathrow), Maureen and I boarded the airplane to Canada. I was homeward bound. Freedom from work and freedom to rest marks the seventh memorial stone of God's grace in my life. He took me away from the crowds of needy people and led me to quiet places to rest.

Aletta and Maureen in Greece 1972
Aletta wearing the shorts Maureen made for her
Maureen removing cactus barbs!!

Aletta, Maureen, and American travelling companion

Aletta and Volkswagen Camper on tour 1972

Trust in the Lord with all your heart; do not depend on your own understanding. Seek his will in all you do, and he will show you which path to take.

Proverbs 3:5–6 (NLT)

FAITHFULNESS

Dad's soak in a bathtub of hot water, fortified with drops of a peddler's tonic, no longer relieved the symptoms of his enlarged prostate. His bladder was full to bursting, and surgery became his only opportunity for relief. Living in Kincardine, Dad transferred to Victoria Hospital in London, Ontario. At age eighty-eight, Dad's mind muddled following his prostate surgery. He suffered a period of confusion and did not recognize his son Gordon. Thankfully, my sister-in-law Anne worked as a nurse at Victoria Hospital, and she kept watch over Dad. She telephoned me regularly with updates, and I sensed that his health was deteriorating.

Six months previously, I had slipped across the Canada–United States border under the guise of visiting friends in Chicago. My genuine reason was to return to work as a resident at West Suburban Hospital; however, my visa application was pending. Expecting visa approval to follow almost immediately after I crossed the border, I started work, but weeks turned into months, and my visa did not come through. With Dad unwell, I felt a growing sense of urgency to make my way home to Canada to be with him. Without proper documentation to account for my length of stay in the

United States, I wondered how I would explain myself at the border.

―⁂―

Working in the boondocks of North India with limited medical equipment and restricted access to diagnostic tests, I practised medicine with whatever resources I had at hand. After years isolated from sophisticated medicine, in February 1973, I returned to Chicago to refresh my medical knowledge. West Suburban Hospital welcomed me back, and even though there was a delay in securing the proper visa, they slotted me in to work as a resident; yet again, I was a doctor in training.

Initially placed in the intensive care unit, I did not have a clue what was going on—having practised bush medicine for so long. When called to an emergency, I ordered what the nurses prompted me to; they knew more about what was available and what the protocols were than I did. It was a very steep learning curve! I scheduled a locum[1] in Cannington, Ontario, for the coming fall and deposited myself back into North America.

Toward the end of April, I drove down to Carville, Louisiana, to attend a weeklong seminar at the National Leprosarium (a hospital for people with leprosy). The hospital began in 1894 when seven leprosy sufferers took up residence in an abandoned sugar plantation along the Mississippi River. A Leper Home was developed,

---

[1] A doctor who stands in temporarily for another doctor.

and by 1920, the now recognized hospital became the responsibility of the US Federal Government.[2]

Dr. Hemwall had recommended the seminar, and not tied down to any definite schedule, I was free to attend. Dr. Paul Brand, an orthopaedic surgeon who had worked in South India with leprosy patients for at least twenty years, was the main speaker. His wife, Dr. Margaret Brand, who was also a surgeon, accompanied him.

Dr. Paul Brand was a pioneer in leprosy research and treatment and had authored books about the Christian faith and medicine. I had heard them both speak a decade or so earlier at a Christian Medical Society meeting. Their work was inspiring, and the opportunity to hear them talk about their experiences and discoveries was too good to miss. Dr. Paul performed reconstructive surgery on the hands of leprosy patients, and Dr. Margaret performed surgery on the eyelids that could no longer shut properly. They quipped each other during the sessions as to which body part was more important, the hands or the eyes.

Following the seminar, I drove back to Chicago, where I had planned to finish at West Suburban Hospital and then, toward the end of July, make my way home to Canada in preparation for my locum in Cannington. Calvary Memorial Church had planned a celebration for me to send me on my way. However, Dad's prostate surgery and subsequent confusion hastened my departure. I missed my farewell party and took off for Canada without saying goodbye to my friends at CMC,

---

[2] For more information, please visit www.leprosyhistory.org.

but they understood the circumstances that called for me to leave early.

With my visa problem unresolved, the threat hanging over me intensified as I approached the United States–Canada border. Having prayed and contemplated as to what I should say, I told the border official that I had attended a seminar in Carville. As my words struck the border official's ears, his skin paled and his eyes widened; his fear was palpable. He leaned back as I poked my passport in his direction, and he frantically waved me on. Without touching my passport, he insisted, "Go, go, go!" The fear of leprosy that I had experienced in India also lingered in North America. Despite research and successful treatments, the stigma remained strong. The Holy Spirit had given me the words to say to the border official, and the deep-rooted and unfounded fear of catching leprosy enabled me to get home to Dad.

I arrived in London, Ontario, in time to celebrate Dad's eighty-ninth birthday. The nurses paraded in a cake with candles burning. We sang "Happy Birthday" with gusto, but our delight was abruptly quelched when Dad's eyes began to leak tears. As our voices warbled out, ". . . and many more!" Dad spoke, "I'll never see another birthday." In that moment, Dad loosened his grip on life.

His prostate had been troubling him for a while, but he was afraid to pursue medical help. One of Dad's friends had died soon after their surgery. So, although

I had suggested that he should have surgery, he had it set in his mind that prostate surgery would be the end of him. "But Dad," I reasoned, "your friend had cancer." No amount of discussion shifted his thinking. So, when prostate surgery became Dad's only choice, he felt doomed to die.

Nevertheless, Dad recovered from his surgery and returned home to Kincardine with Mother and me. They lived on the first floor of a community building, and the only way up to their place was to ascend a flight of stairs. Dad was not long home from hospital when Mother sent him out to buy a gallon of milk. When he returned, I heard him holler from the bottom of the stairs, and so I responded to his call for help. He could not carry the milk up. That was the first time I had seen my dad so physically weak.

A night or two later, I heard Dad coughing. It was the sound of congestion—the kind that comes at night when you lay flat, and your lungs fill up with fluid because your heart is failing. My room was across the hall from my parents' room. On hearing Dad's cough, I rushed in. He was standing beside the bed labouring for breath, and I realized he was in left-sided heart failure.

Since his surgery, I knew that he had been taking furosemide and digitalis tablets to reduce the fluid in his body and to strengthen and regulate his heartbeat—that is all we had in those days. My instinct was to take Dad to the hospital that night, but Mother protested.

She did not realize how sick he was and chewed him out for making a fuss because I was home.

In Mother's domain, I retreated and helped Dad back into bed. I propped him up with pillows so that he was as comfortable as he could be. Any attempt to reason with Mother would only make it worse for Dad. I could not stay there any longer as my being there gave Mother an audience and fuelled her criticism of Dad, so I shifted out to stay with Ruby. It was not long before I was due to start my locum in Cannington.

During my first week in Cannington, my suspicions were realized when Gordon telephoned me: Dad was as unwell, as I had suspected. True to his word, Dad was not to see another birthday.

I returned home for his funeral. Everybody came home, even Lorelie joined us from the west. His death came as quite a shock to Mother, and she suffered the pangs of loneliness that losing a spouse inflicts. Dad's passing planted a heaviness in my heart too. Dad made life happy for me, and he was a quiet mooring, a place to anchor whenever I felt adrift. He had always been there. Dad's nature was to nurture: he loved everybody, and he helped everybody.

His passing also shook my future as the obligation to care for my aging mother fell naturally to me, the one unmarried daughter. I invited Mother to join me in Cannington, but she declined. It was an unsettling time for me as I no longer felt free to wander too far from home. I spent as much time with Mother as possible while she adjusted to being a widow.

My brother Gordon was the power of attorney for both of our parents. To this day, I am thankful for his brotherly love and his kind care of me. Gordon understood the burden of Mother, and he also understood me. One day, he asked me if I intended to go back to India. The short answer was yes. Gordon nodded and said, "It's okay, we will look after Mother." My siblings released me to pursue my vocation and kept a watchful eye on Mother, presiding over her care.

When I left India in 1972, I had no intention to return. Years later, I was to discover that I had experienced a classic case of burnout. Rest and recreation can cure physical exhaustion, but burnout depletes your emotions, your thoughts, and your spirit: it sears the nerve endings to your soul. Just as it takes a long time for new growth to emerge from the devastation of a forest fire, it takes a long time to recover from prolonged stress and heavy strain. Fire can burn trees to the ground or scorch their outer layers, but after the refreshment of soaking rains, seeds sprout from the ashes and green shoots grow on blackened bark.

Although the overland trip with Maureen had revitalized me from the physical endurance of the work in Utraula, the soaking rains had not yet come, and I remained closed to the idea of returning to work in India. That was, until I received communication from Dr. Maria, the German doctor who had replaced me in Utraula.

News reached me that Prem Sewa Hospital continued to serve more people, and with the influx of patients, Dr. Maria was requesting help to share the workload. However, as it had become increasingly difficult for foreign workers to enter India, there was also difficulty recruiting personnel. With more work and less workers, Dr. Maria and Stefan began to talk of leaving Utraula altogether. Without a doctor, the future of Prem Sewa Hospital was in jeopardy, and the villagers, the poor, and the disregarded would again have restricted access to health care. A green shoot erupted in their defence. The Lord revealed to me that my compassion and affection for the people was deeply rooted and alive.

Though my heart was now opened to the idea of returning, the change that had slowly unfolded in India since the end of British rule in 1947 was culminating in difficulties for foreign workers' abilities to enter and work in the country. India had long struggled for independence, and a rise in nationalism agitated against foreigners working in India.

A maze of paperwork and rubber stamps unfurled, and all foreigners needed a visa or a permit. Officials began asking people to leave India. People who had worked for years in India could not return after taking leave in their home countries; applications for re-entry were denied.

At least two years prior to my leaving India, a small group of Indian nationals met together with a small group of foreign workers to examine this unfolding problem. They deliberated and prayed as to how they could sustain the hospitals started by foreign charities, with the imminent evacuation of foreign workers, as well as the loss of foreign infrastructure and monetary aid. The group ultimately formed an Indian-national organization and registered it as a charitable society: Emmanuel Hospital Association (EHA) was formed in 1970. Hospitals that had been set up and managed by foreign charities could continue by placing themselves under the protection of Indian-national administration. It was a time of immense change.

Emmanuel Hospital Association approached me to merge Prem Sewa Hospital into their charitable society. Although our setup was modest, and I felt we had little to contribute, I too foresaw the importance of the merger. Unable to bring it to pass before leaving India, my charity had agreed to proceed with the merger. However, in my absence, they developed a hesitancy and waited for my return. In the interim, Dr. Maria also advocated for the incorporation of Prem Sewa Hospital into Emmanuel Hospital Association as a solution to securing the future of the hospital. Alongside national administration and ownership, it would provide opportunity to attract medical personnel from within India. Unable to see the vision of sustainability, our charity continued to wait for my return before proceeding.

Nobody knew that I had reached burnout and detached myself from returning to work in India, but with the future of Prem Sewa Hospital threatened, a seed sprouted in the ashes. So, as for "going back to India," my first order of business in returning was purpose driven and short: my one goal was to secure Prem Sewa Hospital's future by its incorporation into the EHA.

When I first arrived in India in 1964, I did not need a visa to enter as Canada and India were both members of the British Commonwealth. With this freedom of entry now closed, I wondered if I would be granted a visa to return to India. Aware of the growing number of foreign workers being denied entry, a tension groaned within me as I remembered the ease with which I had left India. With the future of Prem Sewa Hospital in jeopardy of closure and a deepening desire to return, I wrestled with the ensuing difficulty in finding a pathway back. I asked the Lord for His guidance, His help.

The High Commission of India rejected my initial application to return, even though I had obtained a No Objection to Return to India Certificate before leaving in 1972. Unfortunately, the High Commission did not recognize this permit. Disappointed, dejected, and discouraged, I persevered. Further correspondence followed, seeking permission to return to India. Despite these difficulties and delays, a visa was issued, and nearing the close of January 1974 (nineteen months since leaving Utraula with Maureen), I boarded an airplane destined for India.

Days before my departure, I penned a note to my faithful correspondent Ruth, at CMC:

. . . I will not be seeing the folks at Calvary again before I leave North America. . . last few days have been rather rushed. . . I will be glad to get back to India and see just what is happening at Prem Sewa Hospital.

I would soon find out as I entered a whirlwind of travel and meetings, spread from Raxaul to Utraula to Delhi to negotiate the administrative future of Prem Sewa Hospital. Winter in Utraula warmed into hot, dusty days, and I longed for the cool mountain air of Kashmir. After lengthy prayer and discussion, by December 1974, all interested parties agreed that Prem Sewa Hospital should register as a society and incorporate with Emmanuel Hospital Association. Prem Sewa Hospital registered that same month. In the interim, I settled myself back into medical work at Prem Sewa Hospital.

The monsoon season started in April and, as a matter of course, turned the dust to mud. At that point in time, Dr. Maria and her husband, Stefan, left Utraula for three months for further language study and a vacation in the hills. The path stretched out before me, and one wet day, I breathed a deep sigh and realized that I was at home in Utraula and that the Lord had drenched my heart with His love for the people. A lush green had covered the ashes and rejuvenated me. All of me enlivened, and I was back in full swing.

FAITHFULNESS

The Lord made pathways where I saw only obstacles. Without my knowing, He had prepared the way home across the United States–Canada border to be with my dad. By His grace, the Lord gently guided me back to India, keeping me on His path for my life. Being faithful to God and obedient to do the good things He planned for me long ago was only possible by His grace. He beckoned my wholehearted allegiance to Him. Sometimes I strained to hear, I strained to see, but by faith, I knew. Faithfulness is the eighth memorial stone that commemorates the fingerprint of God's grace in my life.

Aletta's Dad, Daniel Bell

We have this treasure from God, but we are only like clay jars that hold the treasure. This is to show that the amazing power we have is from God, not from us. We have troubles all around us, but we are not defeated. We often don't know what to do, but we don't give up. We are persecuted, but God does not leave us. We are hurt sometimes, but we are not destroyed.

2 Corinthians 4:7–9 (ERV)

FRICTION

Before a bridge was built across the Ganges River at Patna, the way to Raxaul (by train or by bus) was exceedingly long and tedious. In March 1975, having just celebrated my thirty-eighth birthday in Utraula, I was on the train rattling along the tracks nearing Raxaul. I did not really want to go. The sun pushed its light above the horizon, and I sighted the Himalayan Mountains. As the landscape emerged, the cloudless sky and morning light brightened the snowy peaks. The magnificence gave me courage to go on. I breathed a deep sigh as I remembered that God, the maker of the mountains, was my help.

While working in Utraula in May 1974, I received a telegram from Keith, the medical superintendent of Duncan Hospital in Raxaul. Duncan Hospital had been founded in 1930 by a Scottish doctor, Dr. Cecil Duncan, in the township of Raxaul on the India–Nepal border in Bihar, a northeast state of India. Foreigners governed the hospital for forty years until 1970 when Duncan Hospital was incorporated into Emmanuel Hospital

Association. Soon after, the foreigners began to withdraw. Keith was the last remaining foreign doctor working there, and he would soon retire to his home country.

His telegram indicated that Duncan Hospital was looking for an Indian national to fill his position, but in the short term, he asked if I would take on the job. His request was emphasized by a letter of invitation from the Duncan Hospital management committee; they had voted unanimously in favour of my joining them as medical superintendent. Hospital staff were accustomed to foreign leadership, and the transition to national leadership was creating some difficulties. (In hindsight, there was an unwritten expectation that I would help ease this transition.)

Duncan Hospital had two hundred beds and a training school for nurses. It was a staggering thought for me to take on the job as medical superintendent. I considered myself unqualified, but God has His way of leading us in directions that do not seem logical, or even possible. My being female in a traditionally patriarchal role would undoubtedly offer a unique contribution. As I weighed the pros and cons, I asked God—albeit with reluctance—to guide my decision. Duncan Hospital was a much bigger place than I was accustomed to. Prem Sewa Hospital was small and manageable, and if the truth be told, having just returned there, I did not want to leave. It was familiar and comfortable, like putting on an old pair of shoes, well-worn in and moulded to the shape of your feet.

During my second year of language study, I had visited Duncan Hospital and stayed there for several months to explore and understand how hospitals functioned in India. Experience is my best teacher, and I discovered that Duncan Hospital was a large enterprise that could not be mirrored in Utraula. Prem Sewa Hospital in Utraula was comparatively small-scale, and the people were much poorer. My earlier impressions of Duncan Hospital had influenced my reluctance to accept the invitation to work there.

Keith planned to stay until November 1974, so I had time to consider. I discussed the proposal with the charity who supervised my life and work in India; accountable to them, I was not free to go anywhere without their approval. The director of personnel agreed that I could take on the job at Duncan Hospital with the proviso that Prem Sewa Hospital had adequate medical staff. The problem remained that the patient load at Prem Sewa had become too much for one doctor. Since my return to Utraula, Dr. Maria worked mostly in community health, leaving the bulk of the hospital work for me. In addition, she had young daughters to consider, and we both agreed that it was not sustainable to function there as a solitary doctor.

With our incorporation into Emmanuel Hospital Association progressing, we looked to secure an Indian female doctor from their pool of resources. Finding a female doctor willing and able to transfer to Prem Sewa Hospital seemed highly unlikely with an overall shortage of doctors in EHA hospitals. If a doctor were found, I would consider it the Lord's seal of approval for me to transfer to Duncan Hospital.

Not particularly open to the move, I attended an EHA function where I met Sister Premi. She was director of the Nurses Training School at Duncan Hospital, and she encouraged me to come and work there. "We really need you," she said. I knew that she had worked with foreigners previously and that she was familiar with their approach. "We need some help," she persisted. "I'll help you to settle in," she said, assuring me of her camaraderie. I did not say too much in response. I acknowledged her petition with a slight smile and inwardly thought, *I am not going to Raxaul*.

During the summer months, I visited Kashmir to escape the monsoon heat. Walking up over the plateau of Dar campground in Pahalgam, I was surprised to come across Keith and his family. He was sitting at the mouth of his tent. As I passed by, I waved and called out in greeting, "Hi!"

He hollered back at me, "When are you going to Raxaul?"

Without changing my stride, I echoed back, "I'm not going to Raxaul." Keith was keen for me to take his place. I had no idea he and his family would be on vacation in Kashmir. The Lord was watering the seed of change, but I was rooted in my current situation; I resisted the idea of moving to Raxaul while others encouraged me.

I continued to sift through the cons. Duncan Hospital was well-known for surgery. *I am not a surgeon*, I reasoned to myself, knowing that the foreign head of surgery had moved to Nepal. Obstetrical care was another biggie for Duncan Hospital with many complex and problematic deliveries—the foreign head of obstetrics and gynecology had also gone. *I am not an expert at either one*, I thought and convinced myself that taking up the position in Raxaul would be preposterous.

Six months passed, and by November 1974, my going to Raxaul became logistically possible. There was an Indian female doctor interested and able to come to replace me at Prem Sewa Hospital, but I said I would wait until I saw the whites of her eyes before I believed it! (Nothing happened in India until it really happened.) To my amazement, by February 1975, the first Indian female doctor came to work at Prem Sewa Hospital! After guiding her through a couple of weeks of orientation, I was freed to accept the task at Duncan Hospital in Raxaul.

Despite not considering myself sufficiently equipped, the provision of a doctor to take my place in Utraula had arrived; no circumstance coincidental, the Lord Himself had unlocked the door. Not without apprehension, I opened it. I packed my bags and stepped out of the ease and familiarity in Utraula toward the unpredictable and unknown in Raxaul.

I was aware that Duncan Hospital staff morale was depleted and that many interpersonal conflicts had erupted—including two office staff who had come to physical blows—which gave credence to the tensions that brewed there. However, knowing that it was the Lord's assignment calmed my dread and my anxiety. Doubting that I was adequate for the task, I believed that He would help me. I supposed that I would be in Raxaul for at least a few months, long enough for EHA to find a permanent replacement. I hoped for no more than six months, but my length of stay was in the Lord's hands.

With my transfer from Prem Sewa Hospital to Duncan Hospital imminent, I received the official transfer papers from EHA headquarters in Delhi. To my astonishment, I had been appointed director of community health *not* medical superintendent as I had expected! With absolutely no experience in community health, I was astounded and contacted EHA for clarification.

It turned out that Joseph, an Indian surgeon who worked at Duncan Hospital, had already taken on the role as *acting* medical superintendent. Even though Joseph planned to move to another place very soon, EHA thought it would be unwise, unsettling, and perhaps offensive if I assumed his position before he left. His delay in leaving was that his wife was pregnant, and they did not want to leave Raxaul until their baby was safely delivered.

The director of community health and the medical superintendent automatically became members of the Duncan Hospital management committee. One member of the committee was appointed senior administrative officer, or more simply put, chief of Duncan Hospital. A greater astonishment when I received the transfer papers was my appointment to this chief position—I most definitely did not see myself qualified for that job! Without my knowing, EHA intended for me to oversee the entire management of Duncan Hospital. Once I understood this, it became clearer as to why I had been appointed director of community health: from this position, I could be appointed chief without upsetting Joseph in his role as acting medical superintendent.

Community health in those days was a consultation in a nearby village. Junior doctors were allocated to attend an open-air clinic, taking a stethoscope and a few medicines. Villagers gathered around to discuss their medical problems in public, and anything complex was referred to the outpatient clinic at Duncan Hospital. I was able to focus on my role as chief since the community health program was already running smoothly. Soon after, I delivered Joseph's baby, and with his leaving, I was reassigned his title of medical superintendent and continued in my role as chief.

Work at Duncan Hospital brought many challenges. Prem Sewa Hospital had become my own little kingdom, and I was comfortable being in charge there—staff thought I had eyes in the back of my head! But at Duncan Hospital, I was way outside my comfort zone. I faced greater responsibilities because it was much larger and busier, and the work was more demanding. There were surgeries and general patients, along with women and children. I also needed to devote time to teaching and training junior doctors, medical students, and nurses. My faith in God was stretched many times, but my trust in Him gradually strengthened.

One of the obstacles to my moving to Duncan Hospital was the operating room. I remember a conversation I had during my three-month rotation with the chief of surgery at West Suburban Hospital in Chicago when he encouraged me to follow in his steps. "No way!" I had responded. Surgery, of any kind, was not on my agenda. It never appealed to me; I did it, but I did not like it. So, when I found myself gowned and gloved with scalpel in hand at Duncan Hospital, I chuckled to myself, recalling my definite decision to not be a surgeon.

To complicate things, the operating room was so hot in Raxaul: there was no air-conditioning, and the temperature reached over 120 degrees Fahrenheit[1]. My head sweated so profusely that the operating-room nurse would tie a sponge on my forehead to catch the drips. Surgery in India was one of my unintended pursuits.

The other main obstacle to my moving to Duncan Hospital was obstetrics and gynecology. In and around Raxaul, women gave birth at home and did not come to Duncan Hospital until extremely late if there was any difficulty. Often, they would need a blood transfusion because they were so anemic. But there was no blood

---

[1] 49 degrees Celsius

bank, and relatives were often unwilling to give theirs. The men believed that if they gave blood, they became irreversibly "weak." (Weak is the word they substituted for impotent.) So, sometimes we used a little चालाकी (*chalaaki*), as we say in Hindi, a little trick.

One woman had placenta previa and was bleeding profusely. She needed a blood transfusion; otherwise, she would die. The husband was a match, but the nurses could not find him! (He did not want to be found.) So, I said to the nurse, "Get everything ready." I went outside and called the woman's name, "The relative of so-and-so?" (That is the way you summoned the relatives, by the patient's name.)

A man stepped forward, and I asked, "What's your name?" He gave it. And I said, "Oh, good! You're the husband?" He wobbled his head, confirming. I said, "Come this way, please." He followed me.

"I want you to lie down here for a minute. I am just going to take a sample of your blood." I turned his head away from me and chatted to him as I worked. He could not see what I was doing, and I had locked the door so no other relatives could come in. However, his mother had followed from a distance and started banging on the door. Taking no notice, I said, "You'll feel a needle prick now." I got the blood we needed, and a nurse whipped it away.

Pressing a swab in the crease of his forearm, I asked him, "Would you like a cup of tea now?" He sat up, and I opened the door. "Excuse me, who are you looking for?" I asked innocently.

The woman screamed at me, "You're killing my son in there!"

Ignoring her antics, I calmly replied, "Oh, do you want to see your son? Well, there he is, sitting up on the trolley, drinking a cup of tea and having a biscuit." He never knew that he had given a large enough sample of his blood to save his wife's life.

With the transition and change in leadership at Duncan Hospital, deep divisions and conflict had developed between the professional staff, and unfortunately, they had split themselves into two warring groups. EHA headquarters intended for me to help bring about reconciliation by my taking on the role as chief. As a newcomer and a foreigner, my stance was neutral.

In April 1975, I invited all the professional staff to meet for a day of prayer. From about three hundred who shared the same belief in God, only ten showed up; people were hard-hearted against each other. Although I recognized many problems, I felt unable to fix them, but the Lord had His reason for putting me there, and knowing that pushed me forward. I pressed on.

The heat came, and my physical energy evaporated. The hot, dry winds lifted the dust and carried it into my throat and filled my eyes with grit. With the rise in heat, personnel problems had also erupted among the non-professional staff, the labourers. People from outside, provoked by foreign presence, agitated trouble against

Duncan Hospital and influenced the labourers to form a trade union. The labourers included the sweepers, the cleaners, the cooks, the kitchen hands, and the चौकिदार (*chokidars*), the night-watchmen or security guards.

The people from outside reflected the persistence of Indian nationalism; they viewed India solely as a Hindu nation (despite the presence of Islam, Christianity, Sikhism, Buddhism, and other religions in India for hundreds of years). Although Duncan Hospital had incorporated into EHA, an Indian national organization, EHA identified itself as Christian, and this was viewed as an affront to patriotism. From within Duncan Hospital, a small number of professional staff, disgruntled with the management of EHA, also stirred the unrest among the labourers; aiming to overthrow hospital management, they encouraged the labourers to protest for higher wages.

One Sunday in early June 1975, some professional staff heard rumours that I was the target of a planned mob attack. Aware a mob was gathering in the bazaar, they were anxious for my safety, so a group of twenty came together to pray; the threat of mob violence softened their hearts, and they united in faith. At first, I was unaware of the threat circulating against me. (I was targeted because I was chief and because I represented EHA.)

When I heard a group had come together to pray, I joined them, pleased with the spontaneity of the meeting—I did not know that they were meeting to pray specifically for me! So, as I stepped into the room, there was a hushed silence. Puzzled, I sat down. After a long pause, somebody cleared their throat and explained the purpose of their meeting together. Feeling stunned, the earth seemed to tilt for a moment, but regaining equilibrium, I held my expression and thanked them for their concern. We settled together to pray, asking the Lord to protect and guide us. The confrontation was halted by His hand, and a mob did not attack me or anyone else that day. Later that evening, in the quiet retreat of my room, I was overwhelmed with gratitude for the support of the staff.

Soon after, I met with the representatives of the labourers. I assured them that regardless of ongoing strikes, threatening mobs, verbal abuse, or any other mischief, the management of the hospital would remain steadfast. The upheaval ceased and all was quiet. Perhaps, the troublemakers had been baffled by a stubborn woman in charge!

Through the remainder of that year, there was a gradual coming together of the professional staff. Key destructive influencers were weeded out and removed. The threat of a mob attack had forced a broken community of people who loved and served the Lord to reform and renew their relationships with each other. Respect for hospital management was reinstated, and peace restored. As 1976 dawned, it was like the budding of spring after a long, frosty winter. The future was filled with possibilities.

In March 1979, Dr. G.N. Golden, an English orthopaedic surgeon visited Duncan Hospital. With Holi celebrations underway, I told him to expect a quiet night in the emergency department. (Holi is an Indian festival, also known as the festival of colours, signalling the start of spring.) With public transport shut down for the holiday, there was limited means of coming to the hospital. Nevertheless, it turned out to be an unusually busy night. A bus accident provided us with a steady stream of injured people. Wanting to travel home to their families for Holi, some people had persuaded an intoxicated bus driver to take them; he crashed about three miles[2] down the road. We were busy all night treating the wounded. I was extremely glad to have an orthopaedic surgeon on hand!

During the night, the police came to Duncan Hospital to question the injured people and to investigate the bus accident. The police brought news of other tales of the night, including the death of two men, killed riding a bicycle near Hardiya Kothi, a small place near to Raxaul. The two men drunk with celebrations had cycled up from a side road onto the main road without a glance at oncoming traffic. They were struck and killed by a Land Rover. Witnesses told police that the Land Rover was white (the same make and colour of the two newer hospital vehicles) and they just kept going; they did not stop. It was a hit-and-run.

The next morning, Reet, Duncan Hospital's business manager, brought news of another accident. He had

---

[2] five kilometres

requested the use of a Land Rover so that a group from the hospital could go on a Christian outreach tour over Holi. They had planned a weeklong excursion, driving into the neighbouring state of Uttar Pradesh. The group was made up of professional staff, mostly department managers, and permission had been given.

Duncan Hospital employed skilled drivers and insured them to drive hospital vehicles—no other employees were protected by insurance or permitted to drive as any accident could invite litigation. Even a minor incident could bring a court case against the hospital. The driver, Wilson, who had gone with them, was an experienced and exceptionally good driver. But, on this occasion, the Land Rover hit a bullock cart.

Reet notified his boss, Duncan Hospital's financial administrator, Frank. As a courtesy, Frank asked Reet to inform me of the accident so that I was aware that a vehicle would be out of action for a few weeks. Reet found me busy at work in one of the hospital wards.

"Oh, I just wanted to tell you that we had a little accident with the Land Rover, but we'll get it repaired," he said.

Unthinkingly, the words dropped out of my mouth, "You aren't the ones who hit and killed those two guys, are you?"

"Oh no, no, no!" With his emphatic reply, I asked him to submit the usual written report and thought nothing more about it.

His report detailed the place of the accident as somewhere near a town in Uttar Pradesh, about one hundred miles[3] from Raxaul. Having hit the bullock cart, they just kept going, too scared to stop and see if anybody was hurt. (In some parts of India, collisions can easily incite a mob and escalate to revenge killings. Rural roads are congested with anything from chickens to cows, bicycles to trucks, and babies to men. Driving mishaps can provoke fear in anyone involved.)

A few weeks later, I was expected in Delhi for EHA's executive meetings and needed a vehicle to take me to the train. A problem emerged when a vehicle was not available. I learned that the Land Rover damaged during Holi had not been returned to service, and the remaining two vehicles had been allocated for other purposes. Irritated, I visited the maintenance department to investigate the delay. To my surprise, the vehicle log of the damaged Land Rover and its holder were nowhere to be found. Where there were once three vehicle logs, there were now only two.

Exploring further, I discovered the dented, white Land Rover hidden away in a garage, with no evidence of any repair. The older, and less dependable, pastel green Land Rover was now parked in the undercover space usually reserved for the newer white-coloured model. The damage to the Land Rover appeared cosmetic. Puzzled, I pointed my chin toward the dent and passed comment to Wilson, the head driver and maintenance guy. "It looks driveable," I said.

He tensed up angrily and spluttered out, "No one can drive it—you ask Mister Reet." Suspicion sizzled like

---

[3] 160 kilometres

water hitting hot oil. Something was amiss! I began to wonder what was being covered up. Had one of the passengers taken over from Wilson and hit the bullock cart? If so, an uninsured driver would increase the risk of litigation against the hospital.

I visited Frank to see what he knew. He knew nothing. So, I urged him to do a little more investigation because, being a foreigner, I would be the last to be told anything. In the meantime, if any legal problems were to materialize, I decided that it would be prudent to have lodged an official report of the accident with the police. So, to make the report, I sent Reet along with Frank to supervise—back to where the Land Rover had hit the bullock cart.

With Reet and Frank away on a two-hundred-mile[4] return journey, I collected witness statements from Wilson and the other passengers who were travelling in the Land Rover at the time of the accident. Without the influence of Reet, the truth was slowly revealed.

I began with Wilson. He was a big burley fellow, and having called him into my office, I asked him about the journey and what had happened along the way. To my astonishment, he burst into tears. (One thing I found difficult to cope up with was a man bursting into tears in front of me. That just undid me.) He said, "You ask Mister Reet—I can't say anything—you ask Mister Reet—what could I do?" The tears rolled down his cheeks, and I thought, *Well, this is hopeless.* So, I sent him on his way.

---

[4] 320 kilometres

He had cried because he was scared. He understood that, as the driver, the vehicle was his responsibility. He thought he was in trouble, and his distress made it clear to me that Reet had not told the whole story. The thought that Reet may have been driving began to cement in my mind. If he had said to Wilson, "I'll drive," Wilson would have had no choice but to hand it over because Reet was far above his rank. I wondered why Wilson was so anguished about hitting a bullock cart: they roll along the road with the occasional lurch, and their path is difficult to anticipate. Even the most experienced driver can hit them. I sensed something else coming to light.

One by one, I called the others to my office. And, one by one, I heard the same story. As if scripted, they told me the highlights of their tour without a word about the bullock cart accident. After listening for a while, I would ask, "How did the accident happen?"

The answers were the same, "I don't know. Let us wait until Reet comes back. He will explain." Closed mouths. No one would give any information, and my patience waned. Not one of them was speaking plainly—there was something hidden in their silence. I could not make sense of why hitting a bullock cart would induce such mute solidarity.

Lastly, I summoned a good friend of Reet's. I knew his reactions well. In that moment, God revealed the truth to me as a thought came into my mind. It was hazy at first, but then suddenly, it sharpened. Reet's friend began with the now familiar recounting of the journey. Again, the bullock cart accident did not feature. Annoyed with the dodging of the topic, I asked one more time, "How did the accident happen?"

It is difficult to avoid a direct question, but each of the men had cleverly sidestepped it and told me nothing. This man was no different, except he laughed when he said, "Wait and see what Reet says when he comes back!" That moment clinched it in my mind, and the whole story unexpectedly crystallized. The floating facts aligned in my thinking: the accident at Hardiya Kothi where the two men were killed, the police looking for a white-coloured Land Rover, the white Land Rover concealed in the garage, the missing logbook, and the silent witnesses—it all came into view.

Sucking in a gulp of air, I declared, "You will not tell me anything about the accident in Uttar Pradesh because it did not happen there—it happened here in Hardiya Kothi. A bullock cart was not hit—two men were hit. What is more, Wilson was not driving—Reet was driving."

Stunned, the man pleaded with me, "Don't tell him that I told you!"

In calm reply, I assured him, "You didn't tell me." Startled by hearing the truth, he imagined that he must have spilled the beans. The truth had been exposed. With this new understanding, I realized that I had sent Frank along with Reet on a wild goose chase!

Listening for their return, I heard the Land Rover pull up at the gate; the familiar throb of a diesel engine in neutral gave me enough time to meet the vehicle as it pulled into park. "Your trip went well?" I inquired.

Yes, they both agreed, the trip had gone well.

Continuing, I questioned, "You've made the report?" Reet tilted his head in the affirmative. Then, I looked at him, and speaking very softly, I said, "Why don't you tell me the truth?" Fear flashed in his eyes and then anger, as he clung to his deceptions. He knew I knew. He grabbed Frank.

"You made me go! I did not want to go!" he hollered. Frank flared back, realizing his comrade had lied—their long and tiresome journey was only to report an accident that had never happened. I stepped in between them, grabbing one arm of each.

"Ok, you guys. You go and cool down!" Frank eased back, and the fire dampened. They walked away.

That night, Reet did not rest. He sifted through his allies. One by one he pressed them to find out who had squealed on him. He was desperate to know who had given him away. And yet, none of them had really told me anything.

Early the next morning, at about six o'clock, Reet came to my door and said, "I want to talk." I agreed and arranged for him to come to my office later that morning. Frank (and a cassette tape recorder concealed in my desk drawer) stood witness to his confession. He admitted his wrongdoing, shedding tears of worry and fear, afraid of the police and being put into prison. Justice for the dead men would likely be carried out in his imprisonment, even if the dead were at fault in their own demise. "Who will care for my wife and my family?" he sobbed and broke down and bawled.

With all that had been uncovered, it was not possible for me to attend the executive meetings in Delhi. I needed to stay close at hand. The situation required handling by EHA executives, so I sent Frank to EHA headquarters on my behalf. He returned with transfer orders for Reet to be moved to a much smaller hospital in Madhya Pradesh, where he did not know anybody. As it was very difficult to fire permanent staff, a transfer was a satisfactory solution.

I stood with Frank when he handed the transfer papers to Reet. Oh man! Reet ripped me upside-down and inside-out! He rubbished me and wiped the floor with me. I did not say a word. I simply listened. He showed his real colours that day, and Frank witnessed them.

The executive director of EHA, Mr. Lalchuangliana, came to Raxaul from Delhi to take charge of Reet's transfer. For this, I was thankful. He was cognizant that it would not have been fitting for a foreigner to supervise the disciplinary proceedings. His first action was to put his name on the hospital bulletin board, announcing that he was assuming my position as chief. A weight lifted from my whole body. He left no room for reprisal. He gave orders for when Reet's living quarters were to be vacated and arranged for the painters to move in on the date of departure. He kept right to the day he set and stayed in Raxaul until Reet's residence in the hospital compound was empty and white-washed. His wisdom proved itself in all that followed.

Although not responsible for the disciplinary action taken, I faced the backlash of Reet's transfer. He blamed me and did not want to leave Raxaul. He was a local guy, an orphan boy who had been raised by foreigners and educated. Duncan Hospital was his home.

One Sunday afternoon in April of 1979, a local politician, and Reet's good friend, came to my room in the hospital grounds and asked me to stop the transfer. But the decision was not mine to reverse. He also visited Frank in his home to emphasize his demand. He was adamant that the transfer could be stopped. In his sphere of influence, if someone was issued a transfer and they did not want to go, at the end of the day, they stayed put. He could not comprehend that EHA worked differently.

He pointed his finger toward me and stabbed at the air. "If you do not stop the transfer, you will be removed, and the front gate of the hospital padlocked within three months!" The Lord sometimes gives you words to say. And I remember my reply, vividly. Standing on the broad section of veranda just outside my room, I was prompted by the Lord; I recognized His stirring in my gut.

In faith, I spoke, "Well, Sir, I know that you are an immensely powerful man. And you can do to me whatever you like, but I will tell you one thing: you can only do to me what my God allows. I am in His hands." He was furious when he walked away.

About one week later, a code blue message came from the administration office. At that time, there was no internal alarm bell or public address system. Messages were handwritten notes, carried by a चपरासी (*chaprasi*), an official messenger. A code blue means an emergency—you are on the run!

I rushed over, wondering what was happening; my mind a whirl with speculation—had Frank had a heart attack? I arrived to discover that the drug inspector had come, unannounced. He had brought the rule book. Suddenly, we were in breach of the law: accused of making intravenous fluids without a licence. We scrambled to focus.

Flipping through the Drugs and Cosmetics Act, I said, "Well, we have not been aware of this compliance issue. Can you give us a week to tidy things up and come back?" He seemed to agree as he was leaving the office. We thought we had been granted a week, but it is difficult to get definite answers from officials in India. That was late morning.

It was mid-afternoon that same day when the drug inspector came back. There was no week of reprieve—he returned with the police, fully armed! They locked the pharmacy, confiscating *all* the bottles of intravenous fluid—except the ones that were hanging up and currently flowing into patients' veins. (That was May 2nd, 1979. It was peak diarrhea season, and at least 80 percent of the patients in the hospital were receiving intravenous fluids. The hospital was chockablock.)

I was powerless. All I could do was stand and watch. The raid continued until about eight o'clock that night. Idris, my Muslim cook, watched the whole ordeal unfold. From a short distance, he stood with me. He was the only one to stay. Typically, when Idris finished his day's work, if you had been late for the evening meal, he would leave the food on the stove for you to warm and serve yourself. But this day, he had kept my food warm, and he had stayed back to serve me my evening meal, well past his finishing time.

Days later, there was a rumbling on the grapevine, a rumour that the police had documented a First Information Report (FIR). Once filed, an FIR initiates a police investigation. Once investigated, the police record their findings, and with enough proof, the case goes to court. The police could arrest me and put me in prison! Looking back, if I had not been a foreigner, I am sure I would have been arrested. Feeling an uneasy bristling in my gut, I knew I needed help.

At that time, making a telephone call to Mr. Lalchuangliana in Delhi meant a trip to the local post office. Any conversation had there would be overheard and broadcast locally. Fortunately, a fellow foreigner, a senior manager from a different international charity, happened to be visiting Duncan Hospital. To maintain discretion, he volunteered to make the three-hour return journey to Motihari to telephone Mr. Lalchuangliana in Delhi on my behalf.

Mr. Lalchuangliana responded immediately and prepared to leave for Raxaul. In the days waiting for him to make the journey from Delhi, hospital staff feared for me and told me that if the police came for me, they would tell them I was not there. I denied them and said, "No, I don't want you telling lies." Thankfully, they never came.

Duncan Hospital had not been an easy place to live or to work. Four years had passed and *anywhere* but Raxaul would have been greener pasture. Remembering my reluctance to go there and the strain of what might unfold tempted me to pack up and walk away for good. When Mr. Lalchuangliana arrived, I told him, "I am happy to go!" (He had given me the choice to leave or to stay.)

Speaking with me face-to-face, he quietly explained, "If you decide to leave, then everything will be okay. We can transfer you to another hospital. But you know, your Indian colleagues will step into your position. And, one by one, they too will be pressured to leave. And, one by one, they will succumb, until no one remains. On the other hand, if you stay, it will be difficult for you." Diplomatically, he asked me to stay, and yet he also made it clear that I was free to leave.

I did not give my answer right away. I took a little time to think and to pray. The politician's threat lingered in my mind. Would a padlock close the front gates? I had a gut feeling that I ought to stay. And so, I did. I stayed to stand against the lies.

To avoid arrest, Mr. Lalchuangliana advised me that I needed an anticipatory bail. He had worked as a district magistrate before his position with EHA, so he was accustomed to presiding over complicated matters and understood the workings of Indian administration and its entanglements. At first, I had never heard of an anticipatory bail, but I was glad to learn about it and thankful to secure one in my favour. With an anticipatory bail, if the police came to arrest me, they would not be able to because I would already have been released on bail for what I was accused of.

The nearest district magistrate to Raxaul was in Motihari. I stood in the same courtroom as Mahatma Gandhi when he appeared before the magistrate in 1917 in support of the indigo farmers in Champaran district.

EHA presided over the whole situation, and as the legal proceedings evolved, they absorbed any expenses. People associated with EHA who owned land or private property used it to put up the bail. Although it was not viewed as a matter directed at me individually, my personal liberties were restricted for many years. The anticipatory bail was granted with the proviso that I could not leave India without permission of the court. Since it was a criminal case, I was unable to leave the country until the matter was resolved. I was also instructed to report to the court once a month.

My brother Gordon recognized the seriousness of my situation and would have liked to inform the Canadian authorities to help get me out of India. To draw attention to his concern, he mailed newspaper clippings of other imprisonments in India and court cases that had needlessly dragged on for many years. Although I declined his help, I was thankful for his caution.

However, with my large family, there was always someone who was sick, and my mother was aging and needed care. This worked out to my advantage when applying to the court for permission to leave India for short periods as I would always have a legitimate reason to go. The court would grant me permission to go home for up to six months on the payment of additional bail. So, although accused and awaiting trial in India, I was able to come and go, just not without a fuss: court hearings, more bail, time, and sometimes, angst. The Lord sustained me, particularly in those early days of navigating through the justice system in a foreign land.

The court case confined me to live and work in Raxaul. Authorities continued to scrutinize foreigners, and some of these were forced to leave India. Obtaining visas and permits was complicated and convoluted. Belonging to the British Commonwealth no longer gave you an open passage into India.

I found myself in the unique position of needing permission to *leave* India rather than permission to *stay*. The Lord's plans for my life and work in India were preserved and continued by way of my becoming a criminal, out on bail. A problem would have arisen if the court had not given me permission to leave India and immigration had refused me permission to stay! The court case, the anticipatory bail, the waiting, and the endless red tape kept me in the country. While some foreigners were being removed from India, I was being forced to stay. God has His way of working.

With the threat of arrest and prison abated, EHA continued to support me in mounting a response. A motion to stop the proceedings started against both me and Duncan Hospital was presented in the High Court of Patna, in the capital city of Bihar. There, the court agreed that I had not been selling intravenous fluids, as the solution was not offered for sale outside of Duncan Hospital. Additionally, the hospital supplied the solution to patients at cost and made no profit from it.

However, the statute itself did not clearly state that *distributing* drugs was prohibited without a licence. I argued that the statute did not actually prohibit the distribution of drugs. But despite the lack of clear wording in the statute, the court found that, in fact, distributing drugs *was* prohibited. As a result, the application to quash the proceedings was dismissed in July 1980. It made no sense to me as intravenous therapy was part of a patient's treatment while they were in hospital.

Subsequently, I was granted permission to appeal this decision in the Supreme Court of India, in Delhi. There the petition sat at the bottom of the pile, waiting for a bribe. A little "grease on the wheel" would have guaranteed a timely hearing, but without, the case sat unnoticed. Due to our unwillingness to contribute to corruption, the case stayed ignored for years.

With the removal of the intravenous fluids from Duncan Hospital, relatives of patients were forced to purchase the fluids available in the bazaar. The more expensive—and less sanitary fluids—often contained sediment floating in the bottles. They never appeared clean, least of all sterile. The quality of Duncan-made fluids was dependable as they were made fresh every day.

In May 1980, permission was given for Duncan Hospital to resume manufacturing intravenous fluids for hospital supply. So, although the court case was unresolved, the hospital was able to continue in its service to the community.

Local daily newspapers began appearing on my desk; articles described what a terrible person I was. One story reported that everyone I operated on died. All sorts of lies. The personal attack was devastating to me, but there was nothing I could do about it; again, I was powerless.

The court case itself was an overarching attack on the hospital's conduct, and the fallout was carried by EHA; however, the criticism of my doctoring was much more difficult to deflect. Some of the hospital staff came to my office. One by one, they came and sat on a stool near my desk and simply stared at me. They wanted to set eyes on the person doing all these terrible things. Daily intimidation and hounding of one sort or another shadowed my work. Constant physical and mental strain pressed in. Except for the knowledge that the Lord was for me, I would have been defeated. Knowing that He held me in that moment and He knew my future, in what seemed like chaos, helped me to persevere.

One Sunday, I noticed a large crowd gathered at the gate. It was a group of गुंडे (*gundae*), hooligans or gangsters. (People hired them to intimidate and create problems, and they were well known for their aggression and violence.) Nothing happened that day, but the tension and the anticipation of trouble left everyone on edge.

The doctors who worked with me were not immune to the destructive influences of the court case. My reputation reflected on them, and they were also threatened. So, I stepped in to protect my colleagues where possible. I often stood beside them in confrontations with patients and their families. I clearly remember one instance pertaining to the case of a child in the pediatric ward. The child suffering with severe vomiting and diarrhea was receiving the appropriate care. Nevertheless, the parents stirred a commotion. The doctor, unable to alleviate their concerns, looked to me for assistance in responding to the parents. I suggested that if they were not satisfied with the treatment being given, they could take their child elsewhere. Unwilling, the parents threatened a river of blood if their child died! Their words echoed in my mind and reverberated in my gut.

One of my junior doctors decided he would make sure no harm came to me. He made his intentions clear by wrapping a bicycle chain around his waist and patrolling the hospital corridors at night. It was an open challenge to anyone who dared come near me. (A metal chain when wielded like a propeller can serve as a threatening weapon.) He asked me, "Dr. Bell, it says in the Bible that if someone strikes you on one cheek, then you should let them strike you on the other. So, if somebody hits me on one side, and I let them hit the other side, can I hit them after that?" I just laughed.

Threats to myself and my medical team were exceedingly difficult to cope with, especially as we were always short-staffed and overworked. Early one weekday morning, I noticed another crowd at the gate. Shortly before six o'clock, I heard them gathering, their voices amplified in the stillness of daybreak. I knew trouble was brewing.

Stepping into the day, I received news of the death of a patient in the night. Routinely, I investigated and reported deaths, but living patient care came first, and so I began my rounds in the male ward. Before I could finish, a mob of angry men swarmed into the ward and surrounded me! It seemed like about two hundred (that is my story, and I am sticking with it!), but I do not know how many because I did not count them. The patient who had died in the night was a local man. His passing was untimely. The crowd had come for answers.

As top dog, it was my throat under the blade. They wanted revenge.

I addressed them, "I am sorry. I cannot give you any answers until I make my inquiry. Patients here come first. As soon as I have opportunity, I will fully investigate and give you answers." They were unappeased and out to slit my throat. There was no escape route. I launched an emergency prayer: *Lord, help me! There is nothing I can do; they are going to slit my throat. I have not done the investigation—I cannot give them an answer until tomorrow.*

I do not know how long it all lasted (it felt like a long time), but it was probably a very brief encounter. Fear has a way of freezing time; it could have been a few seconds or many minutes, but the intensity of the moment throbbed for much longer. One of the men in the crowd, who typically spoke against me, raised his voice and said, "She says she will let us know tomorrow. So, let us leave her now, and we will come back." Clenched fists loosened, and the men retreated. They left me. With fear abated, adrenalin subsided.

It was not too long before peace was once again under siege. Saturday mornings, I held teaching sessions with the doctors. Afterwards, I supervised a staff clinic for the hospital workers. On my way across the grounds, I noticed yet another crowd of people gathered outside the administration offices. Again, I waded in and discovered that the labourers had launched an illegal strike in protest of their conditions of employment. They had effectively barricaded Frank in his office, threatening to keep him there until their ultimatums were met. Their demands were baseless as they were paid above the minimum wage and were very well taken care of. None of their complaints would have held up in court.

Approaching the group, I asked them what was wrong. I listened, and then I warned them that their carryings-on would achieve them nothing. "No work, no pay! Get back to work now or you will be paid nothing for today!" I wheeled around to walk away, but they hemmed me in and blocked my path.

The leader of the pack, an outsider, yelled, "Grab her!" Three men did just that! They grabbed me! In those turbulent days, one of the male nurses or doctors would trail me around the hospital grounds. Thankfully, a male nurse had been following me, and he stepped in to protect me. He pulled me out of there in a flash. Uninjured but shaken, I called an emergency administrative meeting. The men had put their hands on me, but not very hard. In the middle of an angry mob, they heard the shout, "Grab her!" and they had instinctively responded.

At the meeting, we decided to make a united stand against the insults. Letters of warning were issued, and lawsuits initiated. Frank and I left at four o'clock Sunday morning to lodge the legal actions in the district court. Two of the workers who had grabbed me were suspended for two weeks without pay. Thirty of the illegal strikers were disciplined, and ten faced jail sentences from the local police authorities.

Nevertheless, the public and slanderous scrutiny of my abilities as both a doctor and a surgeon triggered an investigation into my professional conduct by the chief medical officer stationed in Motihari. As it happened, I had been sick for several days with fever. A messenger brought word that the chief medical officer planned a visit.

"Well, welcome him to come! Tell him that I am sick in bed with a fever, and maybe he could diagnose my condition." (Neither my colleagues nor I were able to identify the source of my fever. Thinking it may have been malaria, I tried chloroquine, but the fever did not subside.)

While I languished in bed, the chief medical officer came to Duncan Hospital and investigated everything possible in one day, from top to bottom. He found nothing out of order to report, quit his search, and left.

A few days later, barely on my feet and both eyes burning with conjunctivitis, the chief medical officer sent word of a second visit. Exasperated, I prayed, *Lord, I don't really feel up to dealing with him today, but if he comes, I know You will help me.* Leaving the security of my room, I stepped out to face the day.

Around lunchtime, word came to me: "The Sahib has come." With a hushed, but heavy sigh, I moved out to greet the chief medical officer. To my surprise (and secret delight), I discovered that he was not there—it was the family planning officer!

Relieved, I said, "Oh! I thought the chief medical officer was coming today. What's happened?"

"Well," he replied, "The chief medical officer telephoned me, and he was not able to come today. Suddenly, early this morning, he developed diarrhea and vomiting."

With an outward expression of concern, I grinned to myself and silently shouted, *Thank you, Lord!*

My time spent with the family planning officer became profitable for Duncan Hospital. He identified that we performed more tubal ligations than the district hospital, and so he promised additional resources for our family planning program.

With the reports that *every* patient I operated on died, the chief medical officer returned for his final investigation of our surgical records. I gave him all the records from that year, and he could not find one mortality. He himself was a surgeon. Puzzled, he commented, "I know the complexities of the patients who turn up here, so you must have lost some."

"Oh yes, I'm sure I did," I agreed. "Do you want to see the previous year?"

And so, I brought the records of all the patients I had operated on in the previous year. Then he found one. A person with a perforated peptic ulcer had come to the emergency department. The patient died forty-eight hours after surgery. He studied the chart and noted the forty-eight-hour time gap between surgery and death.

"Oh yes! That surgery carries a high mortality rate," he commented aloud.

"Yeah," I affirmed. "Well, you know, surgery is not my expertise, but with every patient I perform surgery on, before the blade touches their skin, I pray for them and for myself, so they are in God's hands." As a Muslim man, he respected my approach, and completing his investigations, he was satisfied and impressed with my professional conduct. As a result, what was meant for evil—the insults and defamation—was traded for good. Amazing.

Music was a great comfort to me. Psalm 96:1 invites us to "Sing a new song to the Lord! Let the whole earth sing to the Lord!"[5] Frank and his wife, Helen, were both excellent musicians. Amid the stress we encountered, they put together an English choir. There were ten of us in the group. Helen would say, "Hey, I think it's time we had another practice." She was a good friend. Sensitive to my unspoken stress, she seemed to know just when I needed to be encouraged. My Indian colleagues took loving care of me during that time.

Singing in my heart language and honouring God transported me far away from my earthly troubles. Lifting my voice in song, lifted me out of my sadness. Disappointment and discouragement frequented my path, but music strengthened my resolve: it was a battle cry. It gave me a sense of victory despite my circumstances.

True prayer is a way of life—not just an emergency way out of trouble. Through my years, the more specific

---

[5] Psalm 96:1 (NLT)

I have made my requests known to the Lord, the more definite His responses have been. In my experience, when God's people come together and pray, God's power triumphs.

With my retirement looming, I began to wonder what would happen if the court case remained unresolved. I had grown accustomed to the rhythm of coming and going from India, with court hearings, court permissions, and deadlines to return. By way of a newsletter, in May 1995, I again asked God's people to pray with me for the resolution of the court case. I also asked the Lord for a favourable outcome. I wanted to be able to move around more freely, to no longer be confined to Raxaul.

Toward the end of that same year, in November 1995, sixteen years had passed since that ominous day when the drug inspector seized the intravenous fluids. I was returning to Duncan Hospital from a sad journey down south to Bangalore where fellow foreign workers had been severely injured in a car accident, and one man had died. The grief and suffering lingered with me as I travelled back to Raxaul.

Entering via the back gate of the hospital, an old Indian man greeted me. It was Sadhu Ji.[6] He was a grey-bearded fellow who lived in a hut just outside of Duncan Hospital. He was once a Hindu holy man, a sadhu, who had become a follower of Jesus. He was

---

[6] In India, adding "Ji" after someone's name or title demonstrates extra respect.

jubilant as he addressed me, "Oh, Doctor Ji! You have won the case!"

"Case?" I wondered. "What case?"

"The intravenous case!" he exclaimed.

I hurried to the then administrator, Sushil. "How long have you known this was coming up?"

"We didn't know!" he said. "They had too many cases backlogged in the Supreme Court, and they decided to clear them all up. You have been completely absolved. The papers will come soon."

The Supreme Court of India's decision was delivered on November 8, 1995. The court looked at the wording of the statute in 1980 and concluded that the statute did not clearly prohibit the distribution of drugs without a licence. Given that the statute did not clearly prohibit distribution, they then determined that it was not a sound decision to find that it did. Although the statute was changed in 1983 to clearly prohibit both the sale and distribution of drugs, the court was compelled to look at the statute as it read in 1980. In so doing, they found that the High Court had erred in its decision. As a result, the High Court's decision was overturned, allowing me to quash the original proceedings against me and against Duncan Hospital. I was soon to be a free woman!

God is a God of justice, and He answers prayers. God's judgment may not be immediate, but it is inevitable. By August 1996, having been regarded as a criminal in India for seventeen years, I was out on bail and waiting. The written judgment in my favour was finally received. I could leave India without permission of the court. I was free.

Meanwhile, in his new appointment, Reet had revealed his pilfering ways and was caught misappropriating hospital funds. (It had long been suspected that he was creatively embezzling funds from Duncan Hospital; however, there was never any proof. As bookkeeping was not my talent, I knew it was unlikely that I would gather any evidence to apprehend him.) So, he was caught out using his old tricks in a new place. Consequently, he was dismissed from EHA and he returned to Raxaul township to live out his days.

I was to discover (much later) that, not long after the accident, Reet had taken the police to see the hospital Land Rovers. They were investigating white Land Rovers in the area, and Reet had obliged their request for a visit. Convincingly, he showed them the two Land Rovers parked together with their corresponding logbooks, one white and one pastel green. However, the white Land Rover that had been damaged in the accident, concealed in the garage, was never shown to the police.

Reet ended his days at Duncan Hospital. He was brought into the hospital in a makeshift ambulance, on the tray of a truck with a stretcher. I met him when he was presented to the emergency department. He was all bloated up. His earthly life at imminent end. He tried to speak to me. His voice was weak with the approach of death. I sensed his remorse; a sad anguish etched in his aged face. "It's ok," I said, and softly spoke his name, "Reet, I forgave you a long time ago."

I encountered some of the most difficult days of my life in Raxaul. The tension and the conflict compelled me to seek God's grace. The friction that I experienced became the ninth memorial stone I use to remember that the Lord in His grace was with me. Trusting Him enabled me to remain steadfast, to overcome the desire for vengeance, and to keep stepping forward in faith. I could do nothing without Him. There was effort and sometimes suffering, but there was also purpose and reward, and much fruit.

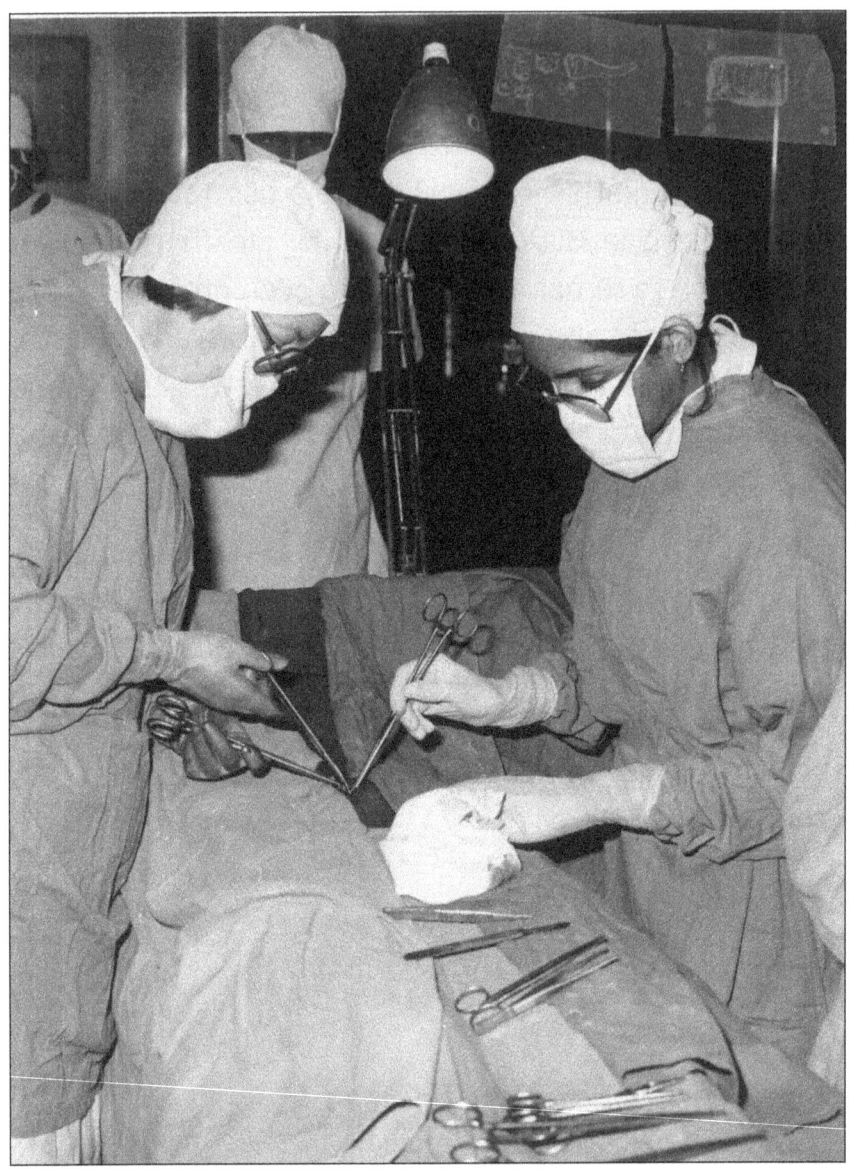

Dr. Bell (left), the surgeon, Duncan Hospital, Raxaul, Bihar, India (photographer unknown)

*Dr. Bell writing surgery notes
(photographer unknown)*

Idris
Cook for Dr. Bell, Duncan Hospital, Raxaul, Bihar, India
(photographer unknown)

[Jesus said,] "I am the vine; you are the branches. If you remain in me and I in you, you will bear much fruit; apart from me you can do nothing."

John 15:5 (NIV)

FRUIT

Shashi walked through a village near Duncan Hospital. Everywhere she looked, her eyes caught sight of oppression. Poverty stared at her from the tangled hair of children at work outside their huts. Their shoeless feet and semi-naked bodies characteristic of their hardship. Girls watched over babies, carried water pots, and cut grass for the livestock, tethered nearby. Early days without play ensnare these children in a cycle of scarcity and deprivation.

Behind them were the tired faces of women: their hope buried in mud and carried away in the heavy rains of the monsoon. Wafting above the stench of rotting manure, the smell of incense reminded Shashi of the Hindu gods. A memory of hunger and despair coiled around her as she remembered her own youth. She had once known her place in the reincarnated stigma of a girl child. Unwanted, she had endured without hope and without love.

Shashi was the daughter of a rabble-rouser, who had been in the thick of the Saturday morning crowd gathered outside the administration offices at Duncan Hospital. He was known to have promoted strikes among his labouring peers. Even though twenty years had passed since those tumultuous days, Shashi labelled herself with her father's history of menacing activities. She expected that his mischief would influence my opinion of her. But despite her anguish, she approached me and asked for a job as a teacher.

Aware that she had worked hard for her qualification, I set her mind at ease. "Shashi, you will never get a job with me because of your father; you'll get a job with me on your own merits!" And so, I employed her to open a village school. The villagers had built a grass hut to be used to teach their children. She did very well, and her work was good. However, Shashi's conduct was not always wholesome. There were problems that needed to be worked through.

At first, I did not know much of Shashi's story. As I learned more about her, I understood that her past was reflected in her present. She was the second-born girl. Her life began in a village with her father's family. Shashi's mother was typically overlooked by her in-laws and forced to work in the fields. She did not make enough breast milk to satisfy Shashi, nor did she have enough money to buy baby formula. Laying in a furrow nearby, Shashi's infant cry was silenced by her mother's hand. (Much later, her mother told Shashi that she had slapped her because she could not bear to hear her hungry cries. She had nothing else to give.) Shashi's father lived away from the village to work at Duncan

Hospital. When he heard the predicament of his family, he approached Duncan Hospital for help, and arrangements were made for them to live on the compound.

As a little girl living on the compound, Shashi became aware of the school there and began to crave an education. But she was a girl, and her future fixed by custom. Her father declared her worthless to the family and refused to invest in educating her. She would one day marry and go to live in another household. He would receive no benefit from her education and neither would she. Although Shashi's family was Hindu, Shashi began attending Sunday school because it was school—and it was open to everyone. Her potential as a scholar was recognized by a Sunday school teacher. Duncan Hospital eventually supported Shashi by providing scholarships to attend the English-medium school on the compound.

Given time, opportunity, and guidance, Shashi's conduct gradually began to change for the better. In the beginning, I considered dismissing her many times, but each time I could not follow through, for one reason or another. I sensed the Lord steer my decision by way of unsettling me; whenever it seemed logical and fair to let her go, I would be compelled to give her another chance.

After a time, Shashi left the village school, where she was working with the smaller children, and began to use her teaching skills in the village women's groups. She excelled in this work through her personal experience of poverty and the hardships of being female. Shashi shared their heart language and implicitly understood the traditions of their Hindu villages.

Shashi came alongside the village women and empowered them to improve their own lives, the lives of their families, and ultimately, the life of the village. One of the ways she achieved this was by drawing them in to take part in adult literacy groups, giving them the opportunity to learn how to read and to write. She also encouraged women to join self-help groups where they could learn how to use their skills and resources to generate income and understand how to manage their earnings.

Many years later, on a return visit to Duncan Hospital in 2014, I delighted in visiting the nearby villages. A small group of workers escorted me on a tour of their labours, and I noticed the warmth of the villagers toward Shashi when they greeted her. As we finished lunch, the group dispersed and I lingered to rest for a while.

In that quiet moment, Shashi approached me and said, "As I walk through the villages, I see myself without Christ. That was me. But by God's grace I am different now." With tears in her eyes, she added, "Doctor Ji, I am sorry I gave you so much trouble. Thank you for always giving me another chance."

In her own words, Shashi told me that she could see herself embodied in the women and children—faces without hope and without love—and she aspired to help them. She wanted to share the hope and love she knew and experienced in her faith in Jesus. As an encouragement to Shashi, she was awarded Employee of the Month for March 2014, and I was honoured to be chosen to hand her that certificate.

The village work began when Duncan Hospital opened a free weekly outpatient clinic in support of the very poor in 1983. This was the Golden Health project, named after Dr. G.N. Golden, an English orthopaedic surgeon who had volunteered his services at Duncan Hospital. The idea for the free outpatient clinic began when Dr. Golden's bone clinic coincided with one of our annual eye camps. At that time, he light-heartedly teased that the eye camp was drying up his clinic because, unlike his clinic, the eye camp was free. (At that time, eye camps at Duncan Hospital were fully funded by a German charity, the Christoffel-Blindenmission [CBM].)[1]

Impressed by the large population that the free eye camp attracted and was able to help, Dr. Golden inquired, "If you had the money, would you consider hosting an orthopaedic camp?" We talked about the logistics. Eye doctoring and bone doctoring are distinctly different specialities. At the eye camps, patients were screened by way of a basic vision test *before* the ophthalmologists examined them. This served to streamline the service. In contrast, orthopaedic patients

---

[1] Now known as Christian Blind Mission.

were less able to be screened or categorized by way of a simple test.

Dr. Golden understood the complexities of his work, and he subsequently developed the idea of a free *general* medical clinic. He secured funding from Tearfund, an international Christian relief agency based in his home country. Aside from a small fee charged for medicines (one rupee, the equivalent to ten cents), all medical and surgical care was free. In support of the project, Duncan Hospital designated charity beds. One man who had abdominal surgery was so grateful for his care that he returned with his best rooster and presented it to the surgeon. Crowds numbered three hundred to five hundred people each week. The Golden Health project proved to be a roaring success and became the launch pad for community-based work.

The eye camp at Duncan Hospital was a family occasion. Eye patients were cared for inside the hospital while their families set up camp in the courtyard and waited. They lined the grounds with piles of straw and tightly woven mats to sleep on and rest. Small cooking fires smouldered among the mesh of people, and walking across the courtyard became almost impossible. (To understand the scale of the event, in 1984 more than 1,000 patients were examined in the eye camp, and approximately 450 had sight-restoring surgery.) Two visiting ophthalmologists from Australia worked alongside Reeta, our resident ophthalmologist. They donated their time and expertise to help these needy folk, year after year.

There was little excitement and beauty to this kind of camping. People were crammed so close to each other, stranger next to stranger, that they breathed each other's breath. But hope builds tolerance, and the anticipation of parents, spouses, and children being able to see made it all bearable. The moment of reward came at the time of fitting glasses. I remember one little nine-year-old girl who had been blind since birth. She had both eyes operated on, and the smile that broke across her face as glasses were propped on her tiny nose was precious to behold.

In 1986, the Golden Health project began to explore and undertake preventive health care. Records of clinic visits showed that many people who came to the weekly outpatient clinic suffered from preventable diseases. Around this same time, the Champapur village council came to Duncan Hospital asking for medical help for their people. Their village was in an adjacent district, Ramgarhwa Block. In response, the Golden Health project began to extend their outpatient services by way of a weekly mobile medical clinic. It was the beginning of a shift out into the community.

Transitioning out of Duncan Hospital to work in the surrounding community was a welcomed challenge. Having handed over the role of medical superintendent to national leadership two years earlier, I had reached a personal threshold working inside the Duncan Hospital compound. With a chronic shortage of doctors, there were endless duties to be done. I had been partly entrenched working in a private clinic, taking care of patients who paid a higher fee to see me. It was a revenue-raising exercise for Duncan Hospital that I had grown weary of performing.

One day I looked up and realized that my patient load was heavier than the joint load of the five doctors who worked in partnership with me. One of the five doctors, a female, kindly helped me. She took preliminary accounts of the medical complaints and recorded them. She also checked blood pressures and any other routine investigations in preparation for my full examination.

Before leaving for North America for a much needed and planned break, I spoke with Mr. Lalchuangliana, the executive director of EHA, based in Delhi. "I haven't come to India to be a money-making machine," I asserted and then continued, "I don't really want to come back to Duncan Hospital." He listened and proposed an alternative. The Golden Health project could benefit from senior doctor involvement with its weekly excursions out to Champapur village. Would I consider joining the outreach to Champapur? I committed to think and pray about his offer.

Poverty is a relative condition of human living. Where we live and rest our head at night and who we look on as those "less fortunate" influences our understanding of poverty. Fundamentally, we view poverty through the eyes of our own position. But there is an unmatched poverty that lays hidden in villages or the back streets of cities that seeps into the bones and leaves no part of the sufferer untouched: the *very* poor. It is the kind of poverty where life and death dwell in equilibrium, and it is difficult to distinguish between the two.

Being poor could be likened to a missed meal—thinning out soup with water, or dividing a single egg to serve a family. Whereas being *very* poor could be likened to missing more "meals" than ever having eaten: scrounging in the field for spilled grains of rice or through the garbage for a scrap to feed your child, or having never held one single egg in your hand. It's the difference between lining your shoes with paper to cover the holes and walking barefoot, scraping your sores with a piece of bark. When the *very* poor become sick, they languish without physical nourishment, with no medicine to soothe their pain or even a scrap of material to keep the flies from laying maggots in their wounds. These people are so impoverished that they are unable to reach out for care.

Although I had been appointed director of community health when I initially transferred to Duncan Hospital in 1975, I remained largely inexperienced in community work. In those earlier days, I was exposed to the appalling poverty in the villages, and I understood that the village was where you would meet the people with the greatest needs. But I had tried to meet these needs by way of encouraging junior doctors to adopt an interest in community work. However, without the boundaries and structured predictability of hospital work, their interest was negligible.

Although staff from Duncan Hospital had started health teaching, home visitations, and health clinics in nearby villages, the overall emphasis of Duncan Hospital administration had been on the curative work of the hospital. When it came to understanding community health work, I was greener than grass and somewhat reluctant to take up Mr. Lalchuangliana's proposal. Nonetheless, God answers prayer in unexpected ways, and without my giving it too much thought, I discovered that I had been appointed as doctor-in-charge of the Golden Health project. As I approached my fiftieth birthday in February 1987, my official transition from hospital to community work began.

Working inside Duncan Hospital, any language shortcomings and lack of cultural knowledge had been absorbed by the walled compound. People entered the facility as guests and were vulnerable to the system functioning inside. As a foreign doctor, I had leaned on my co-workers, and they had navigated me through any language and cultural barriers. Patients accepted my ignorance and welcomed my doctoring of them. But in the community, stepping out into the villages, we became their guests. Taking our work outside the hospital domain, among the people, served them in a far different way. Leaving the security of the compound walls made us vulnerable, but it also made us much more accessible and, in the end, achieved positive health outcomes for individuals, families, and entire villages.

I grappled with the task of teaching village women. Although their enthusiasm was infectious, their concentration was often lacking, and retention was difficult. However, as their teacher, I was humbled by their willingness to learn and their desire to help their community. In the beginning, I was their student, learning how to teach illiterate pupils who had never attended school: a little at a time, with repetition and review.

The overall health of a village can be improved by helping villagers to help themselves since many problems stem from a lack of knowledge, misguided beliefs, or addictions. Women were chosen by the पंचायत (*panchayat*), village council, to learn from us. They were given the title of village health worker and became a vital link as they understood the customs and cultural quirks of their own villages.

We taught them how to treat common illnesses, administer basic first aid, and watch over pregnancy and childbirth. We assessed their learning, and despite pre-test jitters, I was encouraged by how much they retained and remembered. When we equipped them with knowledge and know-how, they passed on their learning to fellow villagers and put their new skills to use. They effectively became a health resource living in the village.

One Sunday afternoon, the husband of a village health worker was bitten by a cobra, a highly venomous snake with a neck that fans out like a hood. These snakes are widely known by their relationship with snake charmers in India; sometimes, they draped the reptile around their necks to transport them. Their venom can be fatal. The village health worker tied three tourniquets on her husband's arm. (The cobra had pierced his finger.) She arranged for immediate transportation to Duncan Hospital, fifteen miles[2] away. On arrival, as the tourniquets were removed, he stopped breathing. He was ventilated, and eight vials of anti-snake venom were injected. He survived. His wife had been able to treat the snake bite with first aid (as taught in that era) because she had been trained as a village health worker.

Village health workers were fundamental to the success of disease prevention because they understood local customs, language, and existing problems. They were ultimately the best educators for improving their community's health. However, in the beginning, the people in the village would only want to seek medicine from Duncan Hospital. They understood that medicine could make a sick person well, and it is what they knew and trusted. But gradually, people began to trust the knowledge of the village health workers. Building trust, in turn, empowered the women and fostered their self-confidence.

I recall the story of one village health worker who questioned and influenced a local "doctor" in his diagnosis and treatment of an unwell newborn. In rural India, there are many "doctors" who set up shop without any qualifications in modern or allopathic medicine. The

---

[2] twenty-five kilometres

unwell newborn presented with very rapid breathing. The "doctor" diagnosed the baby as having tetanus. But the village health worker knew that the mother had been immunized against tetanus during her prenatal care, and the baby was not exhibiting any signs of the muscle spasms as usually seen in tetanus cases. Having been versed in various symptoms and treatments, she thought that the fast respirations were more likely to be related to pneumonia. She insisted that the newborn be given antibiotics, and the baby recovered.

The Champapur project expanded and became an independent unit. In February 1989, a ceremony was held, and the fully-fledged Community Health and Development project was formalized with its new name, Champak. Champak is the English name of a large evergreen tree native to India, the *Magnolia champaca*. It is best known for its sweet-smelling flowers that fittingly symbolized the purpose of the project: to produce fragrant blooms of health. The name Champak was also an abbreviation of the three villages first included in the project.

Three months later, land was bought by the Emmanuel Hospital Association at the edge of Champapur village to build a medical clinic, and I had the privilege of laying the cornerstone. The construction was unhindered, and by September, we celebrated the inauguration of the Champak Community Health and Development Centre building.

A sunny and humid day greeted us. Our official guest, the district magistrate, joined us from Patna as he had expressed a keen interest in community uplift. The excitement intensified—along with a storm that struck the शामियाना (*shamiana*), marquee, moments before the opening. The torrential downpour and high winds reduced the festive tent to a soggy shamble. We made a hasty retreat inside the Champak Centre, and the huge crowd clamoured to squeeze into the much smaller space.

Looking back, in a way, this scene embodied the purpose of the shelter: that so many would seek escape from their illness and despair and that inside Champak they would find hope. The storm didn't dampen our spirits. Four village health workers who had completed their training were presented with certificates and a medical box to help them do their job. It was an unforgettable day.

The Champak team began with a young couple based at Champapur. For a time, they lived and worked in the Champak Centre building. A jeep was stationed there. The husband was a driver and was also a qualified agricultural worker. The outreach began with a weekly general clinic, and the word soon spread. Medications were supplied at the cost of one rupee. A local village man trained in basic pharmacy to dispense drugs also joined the project. And of course, Shashi, the teacher who started a school in Karbola village, would later also become a member of the team. The non-formal education centre opened with thirty-two illiterate children aged between six and twelve years—all eager to learn.

Around this same time, Leela, a local nurse who had trained and worked at Duncan Hospital, moved out to work in a community-health project in Ladakh, a northern region of India sandwiched between Kashmir and China. (Ladakh has been the subject of dispute between India, Pakistan, and China since India's Independence in 1947. The tensions in that area rose and fell, and roads were often barricaded. The mountainous terrain left no option for detouring around roadblocks, often limiting access.)

In January 1990, following four years of working in remote Muslim and Buddhist villages in Ladakh, Leela returned to Duncan Hospital for a much-needed break. Although expecting to return, unrest swept the area, and she was unable to go back to the village health work. Leela was then invited to join the Champak team, and her prior experience was a fantastic asset.

One day, a man brought his wife to the Champak Centre to deliver their baby. Earlier experiences had been harrowing for this couple with the loss of their first four children either at birth or before delivery. They had come to us for help, and throughout this pregnancy, the Champak team had provided prenatal care. Although it was usual for women to deliver their babies at home, in this case, the couple was taking all possible precautions.

Everything seemed fine until the nurses called out for me. I stepped in behind the curtain. The baby had been delivered, lifeless. I took the baby and puffed a cheek full of breath into its mouth. The baby's father watched through a gap in the curtain. Another breath. And then a splutter—the baby's cry broke the silence, and we all exhaled. We thanked the Lord. The baby's father had seen a miracle. "My son was born dead, and she breathed into him, and he became alive!" he exclaimed. Of course, the miracle was not my breath; the miracle was life itself, a life created by God.

Working in the heart of the villages enabled us to care for people who would have otherwise died from curable diseases. Reaching out to the poor and needy, although it exposed me to brokenness and tremendous suffering, was also a source of great joy and hope. A young man was said to have lain in his bed for more than eight months. He was thin and weak with a festering sore on his leg. A low caste Hindu, his fate was ordained by karma. Unable to walk and thought to be nearing death, he was carried by his family to the Champak Centre. I examined him. He had bone tuberculosis and needed daily injections for three months to make him well. But he was afraid. He was so frightened of injections that he refused to come for treatment.

Finally, when he was more dead than alive, he was carried to Champak every day for one month. His leg wound was tended, and as he had grown too weak to be afraid of the injections, he consented to them. Within that one month, the festering sore healed and he was able to walk unaided to the centre to complete his treatment. He regained his strength and returned to his work in the fields. The sparkle in his smiling face and strong healthy body encouraged my weariness and strengthened me to continue.

Sometimes, the inescapable dust and heat discouraged me. The hot winds seemed relentless, and grit coated everything: patient records, equipment, staff, and the patients themselves! We even seemed to swallow dirt! And then the weather changed from a dusty furnace to a muddy steam bath, the dreaded "sick season."

A two-month-old baby boy was brought to Champak in serious condition. Suffering diarrhea, dehydration, and septicemia, the semiconscious baby needed hospitalization, but the usual traffic jam in Raxaul precluded any thoughts of rushing him to Duncan Hospital. Besides, his father was not willing to accept hospital admission. We gave oral rehydration solution, injected antibiotics, and prayed. Three times his mother started the death wail in the clinic, rocking her body as she cried out her mournful lament. Gripped in despair, the family carried their son home. The heaviness of grief travelled with them. Hot, tired, and feeling helpless, I turned to the long line of waiting patients. One week later, the family returned. Their baby boy full of life and love! "For I am the Lord who heals you," says God.[3] We can do nothing apart from Him.

---

[3] Exodus 15:26 (NLT)

Change in our lives produces conflicting thoughts and feelings. The Champak project had progressed, and my title was changed. Four years had passed since I had been identified as the doctor-in-charge of the Golden Health project, and in April 1991, I was then appointed as director of Champak. Up to this point, I had been exploring new territory and learning more about village life.

The Champak team had grown to eight people and offered a broad variety of skills and abilities. Working and learning together, we were beginning to unravel and understand the diverse problems faced by the villagers. We had immersed ourselves in the environment and were starting to address the needs of the people as we understood them. The general clinic attracted four hundred to five hundred patients daily, and we had trained three village health workers who were very active in their village. Together as a team, we listened to, examined, and helped as many patients as was possible. However, we worked without an overall plan and with no formal training in community health and development; our willingness and my newly assigned leadership were not enough to succeed.

In response, during the early months of 1992, I attended a ten-week course in Bangalore for rural health and development training. My head was filled with new ideas, and I returned to Raxaul ready and enthusiastic to implement them. In each village where we were invited to work, we began with a hut-to-hut survey. We were then able to examine both the perceived and unperceived needs of each one. And then, in collaboration with the villages, plans of action for the ensuing year were formed. Village representatives were chosen to establish a village welfare committee, and newly participating villages selected women to be trained as community health volunteers (previously named village health workers). The change in their title reflected their role and purpose to a greater extent.

The Champak Centre expanded services by setting up specialized clinics for tuberculosis, prenatal care, and childhood immunizations. Throughout the villages, the project became involved in water development and sanitation. Communal water pumps were installed, and soak pits were dug to improve public health. (A soak pit is an underground system where wastewater percolates through the earth from a pit and is filtered and cleaned by the natural properties of the soil.)

Fruit trees and kitchen gardens were planted in most of the villages to improve nutrition. Vitamin A deficiency is a preventable cause of childhood blindness, and so carrots, rich in vitamin A, were included in the gardens, and papaya trees supplied fruit rich in vitamin C. A supplementary feeding program for malnourished children under five was implemented in one of the poorest villages: a combination of three grains was supplied, and the villagers cooked and distributed a daily meal to the needy children.

Village women were also empowered through adult literacy programs as well as vocational- and community-health training. Being able to write their own name generated great excitement. Learning functional literacy emboldens people so they are less likely to be exploited by the wealthy, powerful, and literate. Income-generating skills taught in the women's groups included tailor-making classes and candle and incense stick manufacturing.

We set up a thrift and credit system for women. Small groups of women banded together and opened a joint bank account with the national Bank of India. An individual could draw interest-free credit from the pooled resources when needed for family events, such as weddings or funerals. The alternative was using a local loan shark with such high interest rates that the borrower remained in debt and bankrupt. Men also benefited through loan and training initiatives and were given opportunity to improve the family income. Children attended school, and to pay for their writing slates and chalk, they made rehydration packets.

Mahila mandals are women's groups formed in the villages of India. Within these social groups, women can be empowered. Along the main highway that crosses the Indian border at Raxaul and travels up into Nepal, there was a row of about ten hard-liquor shops. They were illegal roadside stops, but bribes kept them from being noticed, and they stayed open. Many of the men who consumed the bootlegger's whisky were daily labourers. They would go out each day to look for work, but they weren't always hired, so they would drink alcohol and arrive home drunk and beat their wives.

The women had been to the government official's office to present their case. He had agreed to act and close the liquor shops but didn't, and so the women encamped themselves for a day around his office. Again, he agreed to close the liquor shops, but again, nothing changed. It was suggested that the mahila mandal groups could band together and position themselves across the main road. Hundreds of women assembled and demonstrated the power of unity. Alone, each was a powerless village woman, but together, they formed a powerful blockade.

Together, they sat on the road, blocking the international route. They refused to move until the liquor shops were smashed down. The government official was called to the scene and granted their request.

Gathering and analyzing statistics showed tangible indications of progress and encouraged our efforts. By 1992, the infant mortality rate (the number of infants who die in the first year of life) had dropped from 73 deaths per 1,000 live births to 67 deaths per 1,000 live births. (As a comparison, the infant mortality rate in Canada in 1992 was 6.1 deaths per 1,000 live births.) In 1994, the needs of thirty thousand patients were responded to through the Champak Centre.

Five rabbits were acquired in 1993 to start a breeding program in the villages as a sustainable food source, wittily dubbed our Bunny Burger program. And by 1997, when the adult literacy program participants approached their final examinations, it was expected that 250 learners would graduate and receive a certificate to mark their success.

In April 1995, a second community health and development project, Chetna, was started, expanding the work into Raxaul Block.[4] The various initiatives undertaken in Champak were also conducted in Chetna.

A Hindi word, चेतना (*chetna*) is understood to convey a feeling or a perception of a sensation. In this instance, चेतना (*chetna*) implies a sense of awakening. The new project name was also an acronym that when expanded stood for Community Health Education Training and Nutritional Awareness.

Again, empowerment was the key goal of this project: drawing alongside communities, advocating for access to local government services, offering skill training for income generation and savings, improving literacy rates, and providing basic health care. By 2012, over two hundred village communities of impoverished people were helped by this project.

One of the most difficult aspects of the village environment was working without electricity. However, energy from the sun became the solution. The more we learned, the more we realized how much more we needed to learn. The Indian government promoted the use of solar power as an alternative energy source for cooking, and so we embarked on a solar panel project

---

[4] Raxaul Block is a subdivision of a District of Bihar, comprised of forty-two villages, named for the proximity of the villages to Raxaul town.

for the Champak Centre building. This would enable us to refrigerate vaccines on-site, rather than transporting them each day from Duncan Hospital. Although only nine miles[5] by road, the journey from Duncan Hospital to Champak took up to an hour. Some days it took much longer, navigating soggy monsoon roads, a slurry of mud and puddles more like sinkholes. And then there was the railway crossing: when a train stopped at Raxaul Station, the railway crossing gates closed, blocking access to the main street (our only way through) for whatever time it took to unload and load the train. Waiting all this time without the comfort of an air-conditioned vehicle!

It was much more difficult to preserve vaccines without refrigeration, and we relied on insulated vaccine carriers lined with ice bricks to keep them cool. In 1993, a solar panel system arrived in Calcutta Port for installation at the Champak Centre. It had been supplied and shipped by benefactors in the United States.

To release the shipment from the Calcutta Port, customs duty had to be paid. The money for this payment was held in an expense account in North America. Unfortunately, the merger with a much larger charity had changed the rules of access to expense accounts, and a once simple transfer of funds from Canada to India became a labyrinth of frustration and confusion. Unable to pay the customs duty, the demurrage would increase daily, until the accumulated storage charges would become unaffordable.

---

[5] fifteen kilometres

In the days before email and mobile telephones, I faxed the international director based in the United States. Unacquainted with the fellow, I wrote a rather descriptive message as to who I was and where I was and demanded to know why I couldn't access *my* expense account. To be sure of the urgency, I concluded that faithfully donated goods were stuck in Calcutta, racking up a prohibitive storage bill. He responded and the funds became available.

In the meantime, I had enlisted many people to pray for the liberation of the solar panel system, as Mr. Lalchuangliana negotiated with Indian customs to waive the added demurrage fee. Following a lengthy wait, the solar panel system was suddenly released without any extra charge. It took six months for the package to be delivered to Champak after its arrival into Calcutta. It reached us in time for the volunteers who came from the United States to install it! What a blessing it was to have lights and refrigeration in the Champak Centre building.

One of the villages we served through the Champak project was home to a small group of Christians. They were people who had grown up with Hindu beliefs and had been transformed by faith in Jesus. An Indian preacher, a national Christian, had reached out to the people in this village. The first person to believe in Jesus in the village was a wealthy man. He lived in a two-storey house made from brick and cement, and he opened his home for a weekly gathering of fellow believers regardless of caste or social class. To encourage the gathering, members of the Champak team would also attend. Together we would sing Hindi bhajans or devotional songs accompanied by the tribal-like rhythm of drums. Portions of the Bible were read out in Bhojpuri, the mother tongue of the people of Bihar.

When I first joined the weekly meeting, I noticed the elaborate concrete likeness of Hanuman, the monkey god (one of the many Hindu gods), adorning the roof at the front of the house. Sometime later, I noticed an empty space where Hanuman had once stood in pride of place. Intrigued, I passed comment. The response: "How can two gods live in one house?" This was followed by "Now I worship the living Lord Jesus Christ, and so Hanuman had to be broken down."

Opposition to God's work was expected and happened in different ways. Two years had passed since the monkey god was taken down, when the Champak team drove to the village for planned health teaching and routine medical care. Outside the village, the road was blocked by a group of young men who quickly surrounded the stationary jeep. Angry accusations were hurled at the team. They alleged that the team had come to convert their village and tear down their temples! Thankfully, they retreated. Another time we visited, the village people threw flaming torches at the jeep. We escaped without harm and withdrew from attending the fellowship there.

Champak moved from strength to strength as the Lord blessed the work of our hands. By 1996, Champak had developed into a training centre for Indian national community health workers. Students came from Bangalore to complete their practical field experience, having trained in the same facility where I had received my instruction in community health and development. We had opportunity to mentor and coach others for similar work across other parts of India.

Mumtaz was a staunch follower of the Muslim faith. He lived in Karbola village with his family, very near to the Champak Centre. He was perplexed when a young couple came to live at the centre. He wondered why *anyone* would come to his poor village. Curious, Mumtaz spent time with the Champak team, and friendships developed. He had accepted the gift of a Bible and a small devotional book. Mumtaz read and asked many questions, but he remained true to his own religion. Then one night, Mumtaz woke to a vision of the Lord Jesus. In listening to Mumtaz speak of his experience, I never asked him what Jesus looked like or what He wore. I knew by the sincerity of his heart that Jesus had made Himself known to Mumtaz. Jesus told him, "I am the way and the truth and the life. No one comes to the Father except through me."[6] It was extraordinary and life-changing for Mumtaz. He now has no doubt that Jesus is the Son of God. It is ultimately the Lord who draws people to Himself.

---

[6] John 14:6 (NIV)

Duncan Hospital has progressed with time. Although the familiar arch remains at the entrance, a new hospital has been built with all the modern equipment. It is so clean and tidy now—so different from when I lived and worked there. The stale urine smell of the female ward has long gone, and the pungent waft of phenyl disinfectant no longer lingers in the courtyard.

Perhaps one of the most striking developments is the neonatal nursery. I remember the old nursery: an island bench made from concrete, moulded with rows of open boxes, and babies lined up side-by-side. In the winter months, one blanket would stretch across the concrete and cover four babies. A trolley was used to take the babies to their mothers, group style, cheek to cheek, lying next to each other.

The Champak project has also progressed with time and continues to come alongside and empower the poor and the needy. Many new projects have developed. One project works to protect vulnerable children from being trafficked. Poor children without the shelter of a home fall prey to human traffickers. They are the children born of parents who don't have land and so move from place to place and don't really belong anywhere. The fraudulent promise of food, shelter, and work easily entices children—driven by hunger and neediness—into captivity. Taken from their wandering, children become prisoners of forced labour, forced criminal activities, and sexual exploitation. The project teaches these children to be savvy of their predators.

Without an address, homeless families cannot register their children in a government school. And so, the project begins to teach these nomadic children how to read and write. The classroom is a group of excited children, gathered beneath a tree. Their parents are also helped to gain access to government programs that give landless people a patch of earth to make a home.

The Lord has produced fruit in my life. For a time, He planted me in India, and through my hands, He shared His love with the poor and needy in places I never imagined to be real. Nothing proves our love for God more than our love for others. There were many difficult days, but His compassion and His grace strengthened me to carry on. Good fruit is plucked from the tree and filled with seed. When the fruit is eaten or rots away, its seed returns to the ground to sprout a new young tree.

It's important to realize that our life is one thread in the tapestry of His Kingdom. Our life is not singular and one day forgotten; it is woven into the lives of those who have passed before us, who surround us, and who will live after us. Sometimes people ask me why I stayed in Raxaul with so much friction swirling around me, but I ask, what if I hadn't stayed? The Lord placed me in Raxaul in a time of change. Change is inevitable, unpredictable, and sometimes, upsetting. But the Lord is unchangeable, and He has assured us that His grace is enough, that His power is made perfect in our weakness, and that apart from Him, we can do nothing. The fruit of my remaining in India (the shift into community health and development work) stands as the tenth memorial stone of God's grace and blessing.

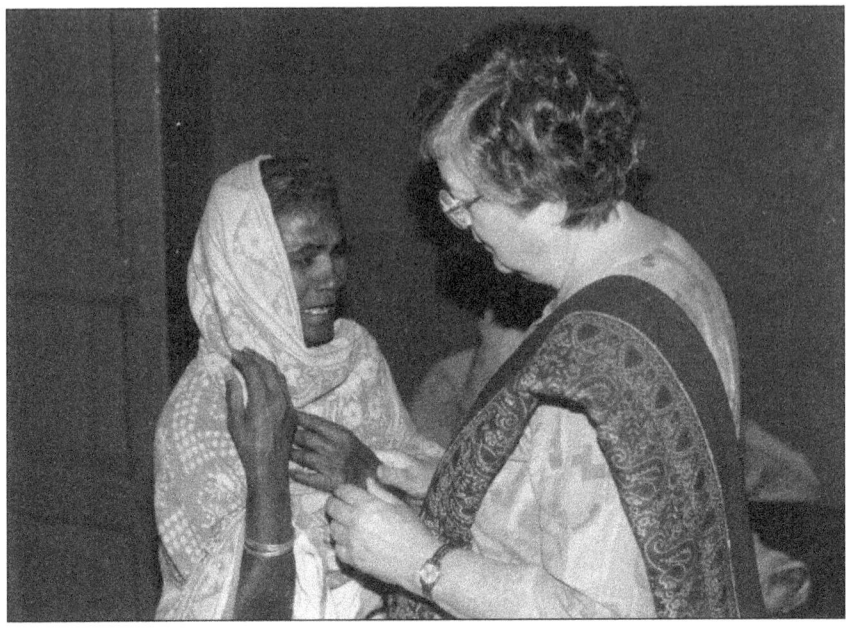

Dr. Bell with a patient.
"Where does it hurt?"

Dr. Bell serving food in a village feeding program for children.
Near Raxaul, Bihar, India.

*Dr. Bell health teaching in a village.
Near Raxaul, Bihar, India.*

*Inside Karbola School with teacher, Shashi.
Near Raxaul, Bihar, India.*

But Jesus called them together and said, "You know that the rulers in this world lord it over their people, and officials flaunt their authority over those under them. But among you it will be different. Whoever wants to be a leader among you must be your servant, and whoever wants to be first among you must become your slave. For even the Son of Man came not to be served but to serve others and to give his life as a ransom for many."

Matthew 20:25–28 (NLT)

FORWARD

Sogra wobbled into my consulting room, leaning heavily on her daughter's arm. Bent over and gasping for breath, she looked more dead than alive. Her earth-stained feet oozed fluid, and the swelling appeared to extend as far as her abdomen. Both Sogra and her daughter wore threadbare sarees; their thin bodies and dusty hair revealed their hardship. Both widowed and destitute, they begged for their existence. Their story, driven by poverty, was one of hunger and long-standing illness. Local remedies in the bazaar had offered no relief.

At first glance, Sogra's advanced symptoms indicated severe heart failure, most likely related to anemia. She needed admission to the hospital. Before I had shifted out to work in the villages, some patients elected to pay a fee to Duncan Hospital to consult with me in an afternoon private clinic. (There were other daily clinics for a nominal fee or no charge.) Sogra and her daughter were beggars, and I asked them why they had paid to see me when they could have attended the other clinic at no cost.

"We heard you are the doctor who talks to God," the daughter replied. Humbled, I paused for a moment. In my heart I uttered a wordless prayer and sensed God's Spirit with me.

"Your mother needs to be admitted," I said. But Sogra refused. We coaxed and cajoled, but to no avail. She adamantly refused admission to the hospital.

"Just give me the medicine, and I will get better," she asserted through huffs of breath. I obliged her request and wrote a prescription for simple medicines: water pills and iron supplements for one week, expecting that she would die that night.

A week later, there was a kerfuffle outside my door. My अयाह (*ayah*), maidservant, guarded the flow of patients into my consulting room. It seemed that someone had barged through and skipped the queue. I stepped out to investigate. It was Sogra's daughter. She had pushed her way through without paying for an appointment. Seeing me appear, she approached me.

"My mother is better," she said. "I need more medicine." I held up my hand to quiet my *ayah*. Sogra's daughter described the change in her mother: she was walking upright, breathing easily, and her bloating had subsided. I was stunned. I had the urge to sing, and I grinned.

Thank you, Lord! My heart called out to Him. Yet another encouragement that God is our Healer.

—⁂—

Over time, our charity's volunteer workforce in India dwindled. People reached retirement, and new recruits were hindered by ongoing visa restrictions. Among the small number of workers who remained, it was thought by some that teaming up with a larger charity would be to our benefit. In 1987, consultations began for us to merge. Even though the larger charity was historically embedded in Africa, it was hoped that the work we had established in Asia would be buoyed up by them and that we would be kept afloat by their administrative base and network.

Our team of workers spread across North India sent a delegate to one of the consultation meetings. She returned and presented her discoveries at our regional meeting in Gonda. Tabling a hefty manual with a thud, she exclaimed, "If we join forces with this charity, this will be our new bible!" But despite our reservations, following two years of consultation and exploring the ramifications of a merger, in January 1989, the amalgamation was official. Our small charity of 115 members combined resources with the thirteenfold-larger charity of 1,535 members.

As the ancient proverb suggests, "a new broom sweeps clean," and in this instance, the merger almost swept us out of India as some of our workers handed their various projects over to nationals, packed up, and returned to their home countries. In the beginning, the merger seemed more like a corporate takeover rather than a combining of two charities; the disparity unintentional—and perhaps unavoidable—given their differences.

Initially, it was difficult to cope with the changes, particularly the increased demand for funds. To cover living and work expenses, I was dependent on charitable donations from a support network in North America. Joining the larger charity significantly increased the amount needed to continue to work abroad.

The changes in the charity paralleled with my transition from hospital to community work in Raxaul. At that juncture, my work life was enough for me to handle, and having reached a half century, the energy of my youth was beginning to wane and my tolerance for bureaucracy had not improved. So, although officially connected with a large international charity, my focus was invested in my work with Emmanuel Hospital Association.

The administration offices in our respective home countries were taken under the wing of a new international headquarters stationed in the United States. Our local administration in India suffered as the merger left us without a direct person in charge. But having formed strong ties with Indian nationals through EHA, I had a well-established and secure network within India to keep me afloat.

An attitude developed within the charity that it was impossible to sign up new recruits to work in India. The headquarters in the United States and recruitment offices around the world believed that India's borders were closed to Christian charitable workers and that the pathway into India was barricaded by red tape. Among those of us who worked inside the country, there were some who shared this belief that our days working in India were limited and, when we left, any projects that we had started would continue to propagate or just fade away. It was said, "The last person out, turn off the lights!"

Not too long after my communication with the international director via fax, the absence of leadership in India was tackled by the charity, demonstrating that they were committed to care for those of us who remained. Apparently, when the question "Who do we appoint as India director?" was asked, my name was put forward. And so, I was invited to take up the position.

At first, I abruptly dismissed the offer, posing my remote location in India as an obvious barrier to leadership within the charity. But after some discussion and careful consideration, I was willing to stand in the gap. However, long before this leadership discussion took place, a colleague working in Allahabad, Dilys, and I had planned a round-the-world trip for our long break from India that was scheduled in about six months time. Putting this forward, I proposed to fill the position up until that time.

Then there was another twirl as our ensuing travel plans were spun around! Our intended travel dates coincided with the International Council: "Could I attend the meeting?" (International Council was a meeting of directors from around the globe, and I would have the opportunity to represent India.) I agreed to swing our whole itinerary around to be able to attend.

The next proposal puzzled me. Before I could stretch myself into this new role, I was also informed that I had been nominated and voted as a member of the board of governors; their next meeting happened to be scheduled within our travel timeframe. I was not aware of the nomination because, without an India director, the nomination and vote had not disseminated to the India workforce. *Who in the world voted for me?* I wondered. *Nobody would have known me in the international community.* Nevertheless, it was official, appointed acting India director with an invitation to the board of governors as a member at large, I stepped forward into leadership. I felt ill-equipped and unprepared for the job.

Dilys, although born in India, was a blend of Welsh and Scottish descent and would one day stop working and retire to live in Britain. We first met in language school, and with our respective retirements not too far away, we planned to make the most of our upcoming vacations. We both had friends and associates spread across the world, and we decided that it would be great to visit them. Dilys was easygoing, adventurous, and fun to travel with. She was also sometimes accident prone and frequently lost things on Indian trains. One time her दुपट्टा (*dupatta*), long scarf or shawl, caught in the wheel of her moped, landing her in hospital with a fractured pelvis! Another time, Dilys couldn't board her train because a large crowd was blocking the door. So, the कुली (*coolie*), luggage porter, carrying her bags lifted her up and slotted her in through a window.

The message I carried to the International Council meeting in 1994 was that India is an accessible country. I pointed to the 10/40 Window: a rectangular shaped region, mapped out on the world globe between 10 and 40 degrees north of the equator.[1] If you look inside this window, it frames North Africa, the Middle East, and Asia. And, if you investigate a little further, pushing back the curtains so that you can view the landscape, you will see some of the world's greatest poverty and lowest quality of life. You will also find the least number of people who believe in and follow Jesus. Today, two-thirds of the world's population live inside this window, and yet only 3 percent of Christian workers are positioned there.[2]

I sketched a map of the 10/40 Window and traced around the Indian border in red ink, located a little to the left—it represented a heart. And, just below India, I traced around the Sri Lankan border in red ink—it represented a droplet. Holding up my sketch, I announced to the International Council, "India is the bleeding heart of the 10/40 Window." Armed with the most recent statistics about populations and need, I tossed them into the room. I gave the council a moment to absorb the disproportionate number of workers allocated in Nigeria, Ethiopia, and South America compared with the number of workers allocated in

---

[1] Luis and Doris Bush first coined the term "10/40 Window" in the late 1980's (https://luisbushpapers.com).

[2] According to The Joshua Project, approximately 5.37 billion individuals live in the revised 10/40 Window (www.joshuaproject.net).

India. I presented the challenge: if you want to reach the world, India is where you need to be.

The meeting had devoted a chunk of time and energy discussing personnel problems in a country where there were many workers. In response, I shared a metaphor about manure. "Fertilizer," I pointed out, "if it is spread over the fields, sweetens the earth and produces growth, but if you leave it in one place, it decays and produces a stench."

The merger had been expected to attract more workers into India; however, this was thwarted by the attitude that India had closed its border to foreign Christian workers. This mindset was entrenched not only in the administration of the charity but within the personnel working in India at the time. People were thinking that it was the end. But India was (and still is) my heart country, and my compassion was placed there. With so much need swirling around me every day, I hoped for others to join me.

My belonging to an Indian national organization coupled with the unresolved court case enabled me to live and work in India, mostly, without hindrance. Legitimacy of Christian workers entering other countries is vital to the integrity of a supporting charity. In times past, it had been possible to enter India as a Christian worker with little restriction. With this old way of entry closed, other valid access opportunities were identified. It was possible to enter India as a business person or as a student. By meeting the terms of these authentic pathways, people could live and work, or live and study, alongside the poorest of the poor and continue in community outreach work by their being there. With this message, the round-the-world trip that Dilys and I had planned morphed into a three-month tour of our charity's administration offices, dotted around the globe.

When Dilys and I made our round-the-world travel plans, smart phones were yet to be invented and public usage of email wasn't common. We relied on the slow exchange of letters mailed back and forth. We also used telegrams, but these were more costly and reserved for urgent messages. Telephone calls between landlines were also possible; although we did not have our own private telephone, and it was sometimes challenging to coordinate. For me, a चपरासी (*chaprasi*), messenger would bring a message from the administration office regarding an incoming call.

Our journey took us to Canada, South Korea, Hong Kong, Australia, New Zealand, and Singapore. It was exhilarating to attend the world's largest Christian gathering in South Korea where sixty-two thousand believers worshipped together. The Korean church we visited was a community of prayer with a large garden set aside for people to withdraw to pray.

In Hong Kong, Dilys and I met with university students to talk about our work in India. To our amusement, their greatest fascination was how long we had lived and worked in India because it was longer than they themselves had walked the earth! Our world

FORWARD

trip expanded my vision and encouraged me through meeting with God's people all over the world. It also served as a springboard to inspire people to join the effort.

The charity developed an approach for the recruitment of workers by encouraging them to commit for a short-term experience. It was an opportunity for us to expose people to the needs of others and for people to explore the possibility of working in a foreign land. I always hoped that people would come, catch the vision, and return for a longer term. My own short-term experience in Arabia had inspired me to pursue working with women and children marginalized from basic health care. The opportunity enabled me to recognize a place for me in the impoverished world, and I understood how my education and developing skills could be useful in other lands. Ultimately, it gave me a clear direction in the pursuit of my life's work. And so, I advocated for short-term workers to come and see: to glimpse the work and to pick up the passion.

Every so often a short-term worker exasperated me. With their limited cross-cultural experience, they occasionally spouted opinions without understanding the whole story. Many opportunities presented for me to reorient their judgments. At one time, I was working on a project proposal to attract funding for a condom-distribution program to reduce the spread of HIV/AIDS. The main target group was the international truck drivers who stopped along the border and used the services of local prostitutes in Raxaul. There was some hesitancy for the charity to endorse the project because there was a belief that handing out condoms would promote promiscuity. They weren't confident that donors would respond positively to the idea. At one point, project approval was light-heartedly hinged on the condoms having a Scripture verse printed on them.

The attitude that offering protection for prostitutes would somehow endorse their activities was reflected in the opinion of a short-term worker. Early one morning, we were sandwiched in the jeep on our way to the Champak Centre. The short-term worker, fresh and interested, was reading the project proposal as we bumped along the village roads. "Oh, this is terrible!" he exclaimed. "Who wrote this?"

I paused long enough for the destruction in his words to subside. "As a matter of fact, I did." An awkward silence filled the jeep as I allowed a few moments for contemplation. "You know something?" I sounded out, "You shouldn't condemn somebody until you have walked in their shoes. Do you know that 85 percent of prostitutes are sold into prostitution as children, often by a parent or other relative? Do you know that?"

The short-term worker slumped back into his seat and said, "No, I didn't."

And to be sure he understood the lesson, I continued, "Don't come here with your holier-than-thou view! Understand what's going on before you rain down condemnation."

Understanding culture other than our own is a fragile art. We often fiercely defend our beliefs without fully understanding where they come from. We are not instinctively aware of the bias of our own culture that ingrains our points of view. When someone from a different place behaves in a way that is not how *we think* they should, a tension arises within us. As such, we must caution ourselves and hasten slowly toward forming opinions of others. A deeper understanding of culture grows with experience; however, we can never truly, completely, and wholly know another—all knowing rests with God alone.

Most short-term workers reported their time in India to be a life-changing experience. Not too many came back for the long haul, but some did, and the India team expanded. Those who did not return, faithfully joined the support teams in their home countries. They increased their charitable giving and prayed more for the world around them than before.

In Raxaul, short-term workers gathered around the evening meal and shared the events of their day. I listened carefully and often resorted to stories from my own experience to help them put everything into context. In busy times, I had as many as fourteen at my table.

Love is the universal language. I've had many short-term workers with me who didn't speak or understand the local languages, but I assure you, their presence heartened the people. The people knew that the short-term workers loved them—and that's the language that

God wants us to use; the language that Jesus demonstrated by His actions.

My last day at Champak Centre, I was sixty-one years old. The Lord blessed me as I handed it over to new leaders. After twenty-three years of living in Raxaul, working both in Duncan Hospital and in the surrounding villages, it was with a great deal of sadness that I said farewell to my friends. When I first stepped into Duncan Hospital to help during the transition from foreign to national leadership in 1975, I had planned to stay in Raxaul for no longer than six months. I have always kept in mind my reluctance to take on the job. And now, many monsoons had come and passed, many babies had birthed, and many lifelong friendships had been forged. A place of unfamiliarity and dread had become my home. But with the court case settled, I was able to leave Raxaul.

Again, having agreed to a temporary position, my role as acting India director had continued until I moved forward and accepted the full directorship. During my seven to eight years in leadership, the team in India grew tenfold as people from around the world joined. We began to meet annually in Goa. At one gathering, we filled a whiteboard with all the connections we had made. We celebrated on the beach, waving sparklers and setting off firecrackers. Somebody had a boom box, and we sang hymns and danced in the sand.

FORWARD

In January 1999, I moved with reluctance to Delhi to consolidate our charity base in North India and to position myself in a central location. I was raised on a farm and city habits were difficult to adopt. Being a country girl moving to the city was difficult. The thirty-hour train journey from Raxaul to Delhi was unpleasant as there was no water in the railcars for the toilets to function and the drought continued at the train stations.

A heat wave struck, and temperatures in Delhi soared to 118 degrees Fahrenheit.[3] My move coincided with the highest recorded temperatures in thirty years. By six o'clock in the morning, inside temperatures measured 100 degrees Fahrenheit.[4] Power cuts and water shortages accompanied the intense heat.

Delhi was a hard place to be, and adjustment wasn't easy as it seemed to take so much longer to achieve even small tasks. Flushing the toilet was sometimes impossible due to water rationing. The landlord of my apartment facilitated the overnight filling of a water tank up on the roof—this was my daily quota. With all the comings and goings of people, often foreigners new to India, their understanding and ability to conserve water was limited.

Another difficulty in Delhi was its density, a tangle of roads, traffic, and people. Venturing more than a few blocks, I always lost my bearings. Street after street after street all looked the same. Before any journey, I negotiated with the auto rickshaw driver the destination

---

[3] 48 degrees Celsius
[4] 38 degrees Celsius

and a set price. Having observed colleagues on shared journeys and having remembered the fare prices between places, I bartered confidently. Air pollution measured off the scale, with the smog likened to being in a forest fire. I was thankful that amid change, I could depend on God staying the same.

I had no permanent place to live in Delhi for the first thirty-seven days. In my fight to survive the big city, I moved from place to place until I found an apartment. It took one month for my telephone to be connected, and after three months, my gas connection was still not official. With the hanging of curtains and a functioning water filter, I began to feel that I had a home. Despite the challenges of setting up the apartment and installing essential services, in those first months I was able to entertain twenty-five members of our charity and accommodate six as they passed through Delhi. I also enjoyed the one redeeming feature of my location: a Mother Dairy ice cream store, only two short blocks away.

In Delhi, I maintained my involvement with Emmanuel Hospital Association, joining a team that evaluated EHA projects and hospitals all around rural North India. It was an internal auditing process, and we travelled together by train to the various sites. I also became involved in an EHA slum project. Urban people were suspicious and much less open than their rural counterparts, and so it was quite an adjustment to work in the slums.

FORWARD

At that time, I knew a young American couple who lived and worked in a Delhi slum. Amy Jo came to me for advice when she and her husband, David, were planning to have a baby, and it wasn't too long before she became pregnant. Excitement bloomed, and Amy Jo's parents planned to come from the United States for the birth and to celebrate the arrival of their grandchild. Amy Jo's parents, Merle and Gloria, were long-time friends and colleagues in the charity; they had worked internationally in Pakistan, Iran, and England.

Before the much-anticipated birth, Amy Jo and David took a short break in Rajasthan where Amy Jo began to experience headaches. Back in Delhi, her headaches worsened, and her obstetrician referred her to a neurologist. Investigations quickly revealed an aggressive brain tumour. As I returned to Delhi from visiting an EHA project, I became aware of Amy Jo's condition. It followed that I was able to be with them through that very difficult time.

A healthy baby girl was delivered by Caesarean, and her mother and father chose her a Hindi name: किरण (Kiran), meaning beam of light or ray, and आशा (Asha), meaning hope. Kiran Asha, thus, in its full meaning, means "Ray of Hope." With Kiran safe and sound, under the same anesthesia, Amy Jo's brain tumour was removed. When she woke, Kiran was cradled in her mother's arms. Amy Jo spoke softly to her daughter. Ten hours passed and Amy Jo lapsed into a coma.

When Merle and Gloria arrived several days later, Amy Jo was in intensive care, reliant on a ventilator to breathe for her. Her brain activity had ceased, and her family agonizingly consented to remove the life support. As her father, Merle, later reflected, "Though thousands had prayed, it was our Lord and Saviour's sovereign will to take her at this time, whether we would understand it or not, her work on earth was finished."

Merle conducted his daughter's funeral service—that would have been an extremely tough thing to do. The people from the slum came. As Hindu people, their expression of grief was accented by long and loud outbursts of wailing. But out of respect for Amy Jo's family, her neighbours from the slum sat quietly, and when the formalities ended, they lingered in condolence. They spoke of the love that they had seen in Amy Jo, and her family pointed toward the Lord as the true source of her love for them.

I remember walking with David and listening as he reasoned through his life with Amy Jo. She had cautioned him that cancer was in her family's genes and that she probably wouldn't live a long life, but he never for a moment thought that it would be that short. Amy Jo passed away at the age of twenty-eight. He wondered if they had chosen the right path by coming to India and should he have taken her home when she became unwell. But he and Amy Jo believed they were on His chosen path for them, and whether in India or the United States, Amy Jo was destined for Heaven.

Faith is believing in what we cannot see. But faith is more than believing in God—it is living a life dependent on God. We can live in our human strength and understanding, or we can entrust our lives to Him. "People cannot see the whole scope of God's work from beginning to end."[5] The Lord guided a small charity to work in India when a way was open. He continued to guide people to work there even when a way seemed closed. And so, I encouraged people to come to India.

The Lord designed each one of us so uniquely that no one shares the same fingerprints, iris patterns, blood vessel maps, or voices—not even identical twins duplicate these things. As such, God has also ordained our life paths intricately, and when He guides someone to a place, He will clear a route. Moving forward into leadership marks the eleventh memorial stone of God's unlimited grace. In my standing as India director, I was able to raise awareness of the needs and challenges in Asia, and the work in India was revitalized. The next generation of workers came and established themselves, and I would be able to pass on the torch to younger hands.

---

[5] Ecclesiastes 3:11b (NLT)

*Dr. Bell visiting a Delhi slum project 2000.
Delhi, India.*

My health may fail, and my spirit may grow weak, but God remains the strength of my heart; he is mine forever.

> Psalm 73:26 (NLT)

FUTURE

July 2013, aged seventy-six, I entered a Toronto hospital for day surgery on my foot and woke up several hours later with an excruciating pain in my ribcage. "What in the world have you done to me? I came in to get the tip of my little toe removed, but I feel like an elephant sat on my chest!" I hollered at the nurse.

"What is your level of pain?" She kept asking me.

Unfamiliar with what she was talking about, I snarled back, "What do you mean, what is my level of pain?!"

She kindly explained the Numeric Pain Rating Scale used to assess a patient's pain. "On a scale from one to ten?" she asked.

Suffering low pain tolerance, I answered, "Twelve!" It was soon apparent that during the operation, my heart had stopped. Revived by cardiac compression, I had cracked ribs and a foggy brain to prove it.

Was it old age or a drug reaction? Not knowing, I can't say, but I do know that it was the beginning of the dreaded last stage: old age. I may have been chronologically a senior, but up until that day, I hadn't behaved like one.

FUTURE

Looking back, I officially stepped down from all leadership positions in May 2001, passing the torch to younger hands. The following year, I dismantled my base in Delhi and formalized my position as a retiree in the charity. The transition from living and working in India to rebuilding a life in Canada began. At that point, I had lived longer in a foreign land than in the country of my birth and, for the most part, without a home of my own.

Any cherished personal belongings, mostly tokens collected on my travels, had been packed away and stored in other people's basements. My accumulation of possessions was minimal. Thirty-eight years spreading roots in India was difficult to dig up and transplant. And although I had visited North America for extended periods of leave, my heart was entrenched in all things India. The people who wholly understood and shared my life and vocational experience did not live in Canada.

Thankfully, my brother-in-law Harry had foresight and forethought of me one day stepping down from work. In 1998, when I was home on leave in Canada, he quietly advised and helped me to establish a stable Canadian residence. Thankfully, I had passed on the bulk of the money I earned while home and working in North America in 1973 to Harry. He had very wisely invested my earnings, and twenty-five years later, the return enabled me to secure an apartment in London, Ontario. In my time abroad, planning for retirement, including financial provision, had not been a consideration or a lawful requirement. The charity motto to "live by faith" (or by what the Lord provided) extended into old age.

The charity helped ease the transition of retirees by giving them a special name: a ROYALL (Retiree on Yet Another Labour of Love). The acronym recognized our years of service and allowed us to continue to participate in some way. Given "royal" status by way of title, carried the privilege of being respected and welcomed by the upcoming generation of workers. Being a ROYALL enabled me to continue visiting and working in India as a mentor and consultant in my field, as well as to act as a spokesperson for the needs in India while at home in North America.

My passion to mobilize people and financial resources for Asia, especially India, gained momentum as a ROYALL. With established networks and the release from the constancy of work, I launched into an itinerant way of life, travelling to and fro between Asia and North America. There was a sense of freedom in moving from one place to the next without the fray of court proceedings or the time constraints of work.

I scheduled my days in India to coincide with the very cool winter season, followed by the sunny and pleasant days of spring. Likewise, I avoided the frigid cold winters of Canada, intersecting my days there with the delights of summer and fall. I attended our charity's annual general meetings, where personnel from across India and neighbouring countries met together in Goa (a southwestern coastal state of India with a history of Portuguese rule and influence). It was a time of listening and encouraging.

Being present on-site, travelling from place to place, enabled me to encourage, counsel, and mentor younger workers. In 2003, I visited a woman living and working in a remote area of Nepal. The rain dripped through bullet holes in her roof. Sheltering there, I sensed a hint of the intensity of what she had experienced caught in the crossfire of civil war. At that time, the Communist Party of Nepal was violently active in its campaign to overthrow the long-standing monarchy. It challenged me as to my preparedness to offer counsel and encouragement. Although I had endured much violence in my work, gunfire had never threatened me.

There was also opportunity to be active in administration, when needed. I developed and field-tested training modules for teaching community health and development workers in our charity. And, for a time, I based myself again in Delhi as a technical consultant to come alongside a new executive of another international charity. My involvement included training others in community-based work, developing new programs, and providing advisory support and technical input for developing training modules for the inexperienced charity. To monitor and assess the effectiveness of the programs, I also helped in setting up systems of evaluation.

As arranged by my charity, I led teams of young folk from North America to experience firsthand the poverty and the need for workers in India: reconnaissance tours for the interested. To coincide with the summer break from universities, when young people were free to travel and explore, it wasn't always possible to avoid the discomfort of an Indian summer. When we stepped outside the airport terminal, the heat and humidity of Delhi would welcome us with a slap in the face. Reeling from the air quality, my "apprentices" were immediately assaulted by a moving mass of people. Delhi is like stepping on a beehive.

They witnessed the mutilated bodies of beggars, tasted culinary delights, and inhaled the stench of raw sewage in the streets. They experienced long days of train travel and participated in the lives of children in schools, orphanages, and hospice-care settings. Summing up their time in India, one of the team members once said, "This has been a life-changing experience for me!" Other teams echoed similar sentiments. Many young people told me that God had broken their hearts for India. And I prayed then as I do now that their faith would manifest into action.

In 2004, nearing sixty-seven years of age, I witnessed for the first time the devastation of the human immunodeficiency virus, or HIV. This blood-borne virus attacks the body's immune system and can lead to an acquired immunodeficiency syndrome, or AIDS. Although there is no cure for an HIV infection, with timely diagnosis, treatment, and care, it has become a manageable chronic condition. Also, as the

Dutch philosopher Desiderius Erasmus suggested, "Prevention is better than cure," and in my experience, remains the best defence in improving the health of a community.

Knowledge is perhaps one dimensional and engages the attention of the mind and at best creates a thought; whereas, experience is multidimensional and connects all the available senses to the subject at hand. So, although I knew that HIV/AIDS was increasing by alarming numbers in India, it was not until I stood in the red-light streets of Delhi that I really saw the face of AIDS. Despair and hopelessness pervaded the faces and bodies of young women and girls.

Through my association with Emmanuel Hospital Association, I was invited to observe a community health and development project focused on providing care and support to people living with HIV/AIDS in and around Delhi. At the time, I described my response as a kaleidoscope of feelings. In other words, when I took a moment to look through the eye hole, I was overwhelmed by the reflections of the lives that I could see.

At Christmas time, I was invited to join the festivities at the HIV/AIDS Shalom Project. (Shalom is a Hebrew word meaning peace.) I met a little girl there; her name was शांति (*Shanti*), Peace, a beautiful child of eleven years. She and her nine-month-old brother had been thrown out of a temple and into the cold dark of night. Their mother, a temple prostitute, had died of AIDS, and her two children had been tossed out as unwanted refuse. In the pouring rain, Shanti and her baby brother were brought home by a project worker from the stark streets of Delhi.

Although her little brother later died of AIDS, Shanti was not infected. The Shalom Project cared for her in their Home of Hope. Her beaming smile and hope-filled eyes reflected the love of Jesus now present in her life. It prompted me to act, advocating for this significant project to be financially supported by North American charities.

With the freedom of retirement, I was able to accept an invitation to join a group of North Americans who were visiting China for one month. We taught English to professors and administrators in a medical school. A weeklong orientation provided us with a basic toolkit as to how to teach English, and I enjoyed setting up class debates on local topics to create conversational learning. We were accommodated in the facility and allocated some free time to explore China itself. I enjoyed a tour of the Terracotta Warriors and standing on the Great Wall.

Aside from the teaching and the touring, the most memorable moments were attending different gatherings of people who believed in Jesus Christ and followed His teachings. In a government-registered church as foreigners and guests, we were ushered to the front of the building, close to the leader of the group, who was teaching. In conflict with government rules, this pastor had been imprisoned for ten years for promoting Christian beliefs and behaviours. (The Chinese government regulated religious practices to prevent any disloyalty or undermining of their leadership.)

The church itself was an old building, lined with the familiar wooden pews that I was accustomed to. The music was unhindered, and I remember that I was able to join in the singing. Although we were free to sing, there was a strong sense of being watched very closely. It was like being given the freedom to live in a cage.

By invitation, I also attended an underground church meeting. (The underground church refers to an illegal gathering of believers not registered or regulated by the government.) We met in an apartment. It is customary to remove your shoes and leave them outside the door, but to avoid detection, everyone picked up their shoes and placed them inside the door, concealing their presence. The room was cleared of furniture and an oriental-patterned rug covered the floor. About thirty to forty people sat together. No music or singing was possible.

Several people spoke about their faith journey, either the moment they believed in Jesus or their most recent experiences in following Him. The people prayed together, and there didn't appear to be a designated leader or teacher who spoke. It felt like a cohesive group of believers who couldn't expose themselves. They were bonded in preserving their meeting place so that they could come together to worship God without the control of the authorities.

As an outsider, unfamiliar with local culture and custom, I could not see a difference in the core beliefs between the registered church and the underground church. In both, the way of salvation was there: the death of Jesus and God raising Jesus to life. However, I glimpsed the lack of freedom to express your faith in your everyday life without fear of harassment, oppression, or maltreatment by the government. Being a Jesus follower was viewed as a threat to the status quo of the socialist administration. It reminded me of other lands where you do not have to hide your faith—but you also cannot share it openly.

Living in India, I shared my faith through the work of my hands and by my being there. In the intrigue of being foreign, there was often an acceptance of a different faith, or an expectation that I would be a Christian. The Hindu religion embraces a plethora of gods, and appeasing deities is commonplace; there is an openness to the spiritual realms and dimensions. The animation of my life openly proclaimed my beliefs; it was not possible to hide it.

While in North America, I travelled widely to tell people about the needs in other lands. In 2006 alone, I drove some fifteen thousand miles[1] throughout Ontario, across Western Canada to Vancouver, and down through the United States to Chicago, interacting with young people in Bible colleges, universities, and churches. I began to see a change in the outlook of the

---

[1] 24,140 kilometres

generation following me. The world that influenced me was not the same world that had shaped them. There had been a significant shift in the values, principles, and beliefs since I was young. Ideas and behaviours that had once been unspoken and hidden had become unrestricted, and what was once forbidden was permissible. But a change in the world system does not reflect a change in the needs of people, and much less in the heart of God.

On one of my many ROYALL visits to Delhi, I discovered the leadership team exhausted and unwell, and I quickly became immersed in many tasks. For one month, I volunteered as acting India director to allow the incumbent to take a much-needed break. The personnel director had also resigned, and another member of staff was waiting in Toronto for a visa. I visited many members of the team on-site and offered pastoral care.

Our charity also ran a transit house for incoming and outgoing personnel and visitors. An Indian couple had been employed to manage the transit house; however, they were several months from arriving, and so I based myself there during the day to oversee the comings and goings. This also involved providing orientation to short-term associates, including teams, and carrying out their debrief. At age seventy, life was very full—and exhausting—at times.

I became increasingly aware of a need for skilled pastoral care and counsel to ensure the physical, emotional, and spiritual welfare of those who came after me. So, in 2009, realizing that my old brain needed a bit of stimulus and new knowledge, I enrolled in a counselling course at Heritage College and Seminary in Cambridge, Ontario. I had planned to complete a Master of Divinity in Counselling by my eightieth birthday, but the program was withdrawn from the curriculum when I was three-quarters through. Nonetheless, the teaching and learning were not wasted in my interactions with others or in my own pilgrimage.

In 2011, the international nature of the charity opened an opportunity for me to temporarily cover leave as an area director. The position was based in Thailand and coordinated work in Nepal, the Philippines, China, and Mongolia. When I visited Mongolia, I was inspired by the work being undertaken among the nomads dwelling in their yurts. (A yurt is a sturdy type of round tent.) The landscape and the continued existence of the people captivated me. Unfortunately, the influences of city life had long since been unravelling the old ways. A once subsistent livelihood had morphed into a life of poverty. Disease, sickness, and injuries maimed the once romantic nomadic wheel of life.

I witnessed the work of a Christian medical agricultural organization providing medicine and veterinary care for their animals. I imagined piggybacking a community health outreach to meet the human needs. With the knowledge gained on the job in cross-cultural work, I itched to continue in this ancient land. My travel companions invited me to come, "You come and do it—do what you suggest!" For a moment, the desire rose in my heart and mind but soon dampened in the body of my old age. Besides, I didn't speak the language of the people there. Even now as I remember Mongolia, enthusiasm buds for what could be achieved if others were willing.

The years of *retirement* rolled by. I have italicized the word *retirement* as its true meaning indicates a departure, a leaving, and a withdrawal. It is, essentially, stepping down and giving up work. But when I stepped down from leadership and formally withdrew from my everyday work, I didn't pull the bus into park and turn off the engine. Conversely, the bus was fully loaded with a lifetime of experience, and so I pulled out onto the highway and accelerated into *retirement*.

But every part of retirement hasn't been filled with labour and work. There have been many good times of much needed and much appreciated rest. One wonderful week, I lounged with friends from India and Nepal on a beach in the Gulf of Thailand, soaked in the warmth of the sea, and ambled along the coast. At age seventy-four, the refreshment of that week made me more aware of the fatigue and weariness of constant travel and work. It somehow prepared me to face up to my first Canadian winter in over forty years.

During one of my in person modules at Heritage College and Seminary, I stayed with my childhood friend Faith for a week. In renewing the friendship of our youth, Faith talked about a cottage in Georgian Bay, on one of the Great Lakes: Lake Huron. She invited me to join her there in the summer. For several years, Faith treated me to wonderful weeks of refreshment on a small island. Woken with the warm colours of sunrise most days, I slipped into the cool water for a float on my pool noodle. Paddling well out of my depth, the buoyancy of the foam kept my head suspended above the water—I have never learned how to swim and keep myself afloat. I disconnected from all communications, and the world suddenly stopped. The stillness of our days, the quiet calm, and the togetherness rested the whole of me. Our days would close with the eerie hoots of a loon family coming in to feed at dusk.

Another blessing was the spectacular and unforgettable experience of the Tournament of Roses Parade in Pasadena. This New Year's Day parade is a festival of flowers unique to California. My dream to set eyes on—and to inhale the sweet aromas of—the parade welcomed 2013 with excitement and awe. Young friends Kim and Troy who had worked in India arranged the expedition, including a close-up view of the floats the day before the parade. We had a behind-the-scenes glimpse of the construction of the platforms, decorated and covered in masses of fresh flowers.

As I reached my retirement, my older siblings reached their old age. My siblings were a mainstay throughout my years of work abroad—always there to come home to, always there to buoy me up. As adults we enjoyed vacations together, and as I learned more about them, I became even more grateful for them than I had been as a child. My sister Ruby was the first of us girls to pass away. Having managed insulin-dependent diabetes for most of her adult years, she died twelve days after her eighty-second birthday. Her passing stirred the familiar unease of grief, and an unspoken sadness settled in my heart. On the third Christmas that followed, I enjoyed celebrations with my family. Ruby's absence reminded me of the preciousness of my family, and I paused to thank God for the constant support and encouragement shown to me.

As much as possible, I visited my aging siblings spread across Canada from Vancouver in the West to Toronto in the East. Sometimes my siblings were ailing, and other times they were not much longer for this world. But one of the best times I remember was in July 2013, when I drove Dorothy and Sheila to Palmerston, Ontario, to celebrate our older sister Effie's ninety-fifth birthday. A cherished memory that then reminded me of the brevity of this earthly life. As the years have passed, all my eight siblings have passed from the ills and constraints of being elderly into the wonder of their eternal home. On occasion, I have been privileged to deliver a eulogy in honour of them.

As a follower of Jesus, I have always been thankful to belong to God's family. His family is worldwide and embraces a plethora of customs and points of view. Moving back to Canada to replant in the country of my birth was testing and difficult at times. Navigating new relationships and restoring old ones isn't easy when most of your life has been shaped and influenced in another nation. You can't pick up where you left off because a lifetime has passed, and many things about your home country have become strange and unfamiliar. You grieve the country of your heart, the place where you invested your life's work, and nobody around you can see your longing to go home because they think you're already there.

Finding a church to embed myself in, to fellowship with others who also loved and served Jesus, was vital for me through this period of change, and to live out my earth-bound years. Having worked with an interfaith charity for most of my life produced a practical challenge as I searched for a home amid the denominational structure of the churches in Canada. But I needed to belong to a local community and was soon welcomed into one.

As another decade of my life was ending and my becoming an octogenarian was imminent, one of the most thrilling blessings unfolded. In November 2016, by way of invitation, I returned to Utraula to celebrate the fiftieth anniversary of Prem Sewa Hospital. Kim and her youngest daughter, Asha, travelled with me from Delhi. Eileen and Dilys, work comrades and lifelong friends, arrived from their homes in England, and Dr. Maria and her husband, Stefan, came from Germany.

FUTURE

We were royally welcomed with garlands of flowers. Five days of celebrations ensued, with the main event held under an elaborate शामियाना (*shamiana*), marquee. At least eight hundred people gathered for the occasion.

The little seed that was planted had grown. Prem Sewa Hospital had flourished through the hands of nationals—the Indian people themselves—who cared for the poor and marginalized in their home country. Fifty years of *Loving Service* commemorated over a week of festivities was a delight to take part in. I had the honour of cutting a ribbon to formally open the new eye department. Having founded and worked in the hospital, I was blessed to see what God achieved through our hands.

The high note of the jubilee celebrations in Utraula has come to mark my most recent trip to India. The transition into my eighties was a roller-coaster ride with frequent ups and downs as I encountered one bend in the road after another. My eighty-year-old body had difficulty keeping up with all the adventures. Changes in health and physical strength seemed sudden, and everyday jobs began to take *all* day! And then, a virus swept the world, and for one entire year I stayed locked down to keep safe.

Through these years, I have not been alone as Nicky came to be with me to write my story. Although she has helped me to navigate life as an elder, it remains a challenge for me to be on the other side of medicine. It is preferable to be on the side that's offering the help and healing. For me, as a retired doctor, to be the recipient of medical care has been a rough and unpleasant journey. The trauma of emergency department visits and so many medical people examining my body without time to listen to me, to know me, and to understand me has not been easy. But as my body has grown tired and slow, my spirit has strengthened and soars closer to Heaven. Through physical changes and suffering, the Lord continues to teach me patience and perseverance.

Reaching old age is the twelfth memorial stone of grace. In the eighty-eight-year span of my life, the most important lesson has been that every time I came to the end of myself, the Lord began something amazing. What do these stones mean? Each stone dependent on the other, like bricks in a wall, is a tangible reminder of God's grace toward me. In His grace, by His grace, and through His grace, I have lived and continue to live. He has given me longevity and a future. God gives us our first breath and every other breath that follows. And when our earthly bodies die, if we believe in Him, we will live with Him in Heaven, forever.

He designed us to be so wonderful and complex that we never fully understand ourselves. He gave us a will and a mind for our own choosing. Our life on earth is ours to live. While we are here, God asks us to believe in Him. He longs for us to turn toward Him. His heart's desire is for us to accept His gift of eternal life, given freely to us through the death and resurrection of His

Son, Jesus. Through the Holy Spirit, may you know Him and walk with Him. God uses the most unlikely people in this world to do the impossible, if we are willing.

> God saved you by his grace when you believed. And you can't take credit for this; it is a gift from God. Salvation is not a reward for the good things we have done, so none of us can boast about it.
>
> Ephesians 2:8–9 (NLT)

Dr. Bell retirement, aged 65

*Dr. Bell
Kashmir, India.*

www.ingramcontent.com/pod-product-compliance
Lightning Source LLC
Chambersburg PA
CBHW032033150426
43194CB00006B/263